T 32328

L

D0005343

WOMEN
OF THE SEA

Ten Pirate Stories

WOMEN
OF THE SEA
Ten Pirate Stories

Myra Weatherly

MORGAN
REYNOLDS
PUBLISHING
Greensboro, North Carolina

Ynes Mexia

Women of the Sea

Women of the Wind

Women
Adventurers

WOMEN OF THE SEA: TEN PIRATE STORIES

Copyright © 2006 by Myra Weatherly

All rights reserved.
This book, or parts thereof, may not be reproduced in any form
except by written consent of the publisher. For more information write:
Morgan Reynolds Publishing, Inc., 620 South Elm Street, Suite 223
Greensboro, North Carolina 27406 USA

For Pam and Marcia

Library of Congress Cataloging-in-Publication Data

Weatherly, Myra.
    Women of the sea : ten pirate stories / Myra Weatherly.— 1st ed.
        p. cm.
Includes bibliographical references and index.
    ISBN-13: 978-1-931798-80-8 (library binding)
    ISBN-10: 1-931798-80-X (library binding)
    1. Women pirates—Biography. 2. Pirates—Biography. I. Title.
    G535.W398 2006
    910.4'5—dc22

                            2005022631

Printed in the United States of America
First Edition

CONTENTS

Introduction 8

Alfhild 11

Grace O'Malley 21

Lady Killigrew 37

Maria Cobham 51

Mary Read 63

Anne Bonny 77

Rachel Wall 93

Fanny Campbell 107

Cheng I Sao 121

Lai Choi San 135

Glossary 146
Sources 148
Bibliography 155
Web sites 158
Index 159

INTRODUCTION

With pitch and tar her hands were hard
Tho' once like velvet soft
She weighed the anchor, heav'd the lead
And boldly went aloft.

From a traditional Nova Scotia ballad,
"Female Sailor Bold"

Pirate! When you hear the word, you probably think of *men* roaming the high seas, searching for ships to plunder. Yet, there were *women* pirates. They sailed, robbed, and fought. Some of the fiercest, cruelest, and most daring pirates who ever lived were women.

Piracy has existed since the earliest times. Homer's epic poems, written more than 4,000 years ago, include references to piracy. Around 79 BCE, Greek pirates seized a young Roman noble, Julius Caesar. He paid the pirates a large ransom for his release. Later, he captured and crucified them.

Alfhild is the first woman pirate to appear in the pages of history. Her father was a Scandinavian king in the fifth century. Although this story of a royal lady seeking adventure on the high seas has the air of myth about it, the characters were some of the early rulers of Denmark. During the Middle Ages, the Vikings—Scandinavian seafarers—in their dragon-headed ships plundered far afield, ravaging the coasts of Europe. Beginning in the 1200s, pirates and smugglers caused enormous havoc off the southern shores of England.

An intensive period of piracy began in the Western world in the 1650s and ended around 1725. The last thirty-three years of this period of plundering earned the name the Golden Age of Piracy. The scene shifted to the Orient in the early nineteenth century as pirates scourged the China seas. An exceptional woman called Cheng I Sao commanded a fleet of 2,000 junks and 70,000 men and women. Surprising as it may seem, piracy still flourishes in some parts of the world today.

In the panorama of pirate history, women are few. Stripped of glamorizing myths, the true story of women pirates emerges. Authenticated records tell tales of romance, brutality, and intrigue that are often far more compelling than fiction. Their names are not well known, but women pirates left their mark upon history.

Each of the riveting stories presented here differs. Accounts of this bold, brutal breed of women have a common thread: each chose an adventurous, defiant lifestyle that broke out of old patterns and forged new paths.

Who they were, what they did, and how they did it continues to capture our imagination.

ALFHILD

Princess Pirate

Alfhild, daughter of the Viking king Siward, is the first woman pirate to appear in the pages of history. Her story was already hundreds of years old when Saxo Grammaticus, medieval historian of Denmark, recorded it in the twelfth century.

No one can be certain how much of her story is true because medieval historians often wove myth and history together, gleaning information from old songs, runic inscriptions, and tradition. However implausible Alfhild's story may seem, certain aspects of it are rooted in fact: the characters are some of the early rulers of Denmark, and piracy did exist in the Middle Ages in Scandinavia—what is now Denmark, Norway, and Sweden.

Some four hundred years after the decline of the Roman Empire, Viking ships began making forays into the frigid waters of the North Sea. Overcrowding and famine are the most likely reasons behind the sudden increase in Scandinavian pirate attacks. Life was harsh: the soil unresponsive and the weather unrelenting.

Whenever the fishing was not going well, these Norse pirates set out on long-distance pillaging and colonizing expeditions, navigating by the sun, moon, and stars, which were often hidden behind massive cloud banks, making them unreliable guides. There were no maps, charts, lighthouses, compasses, or foghorns. A lack of instruments forced the Norsemen to hug the coast wherever possible. They were early masters of "island hopping."

The monasteries of Ireland, England, and France were treasure houses of gold and silver ornaments, jewels, and glittering brocades. They seemed to offer almost limitless bounty to the northern pirates from a stark land.

A single shipload of spoils was enough to unleash an avalanche of greed that initiated centuries of wild and adventurous cold-blooded piracy. In Viking society, thievery was considered an honorable occupation and fighting reigned supreme. Children's games were actually lessons in warfare. Youngsters were trained to thrust a sword, swing a battle-ax, and throw a spear. Jumping, running, wrestling, skating, skiing, swimming, rowing, and horseback riding ensured the development of strong bodies.

These fearless and skilled raiders from the north carried out barbaric acts in the name of the Viking gods, their allies in any bloody fracas. Only by death in battle could a Norseman enter Valhalla, the warrior's heaven.

Not only did the unrelenting and mobile sea rovers ransack wealthy targets, they invaded towns and villages on the coasts of Ireland, England, Scotland, France, Spain, North Africa, and Italy. They would row up the Thames or the Loire in their sleek, swift dragon ships, like a swarm of dark red seabirds, and prey on the countryside—stealing horses, burning, killing, looting— and vanish before anyone could take action.

The Norse marauders sailed down the river systems to the Black Sea into what is now Russia, leaving a trail of plundered towns. Eventually, their brilliantly striped sails appeared in Constantinople, where the Byzantine emperor enlisted the towering fair-haired pirates, with their insatiable appetites for drunkenness, gluttony, and brawls, as his bodyguards. They became the Varangers, a corps of regal strongmen who terrified the empire as far afield as Alexandria and upper Egypt.

In this seafaring area, there must have been women who answered the beckoning call of the sea. Saxo wanted to impress upon his readers that women pirates were real, and so he told the story of Alfhild.

He wrote, "There were some women among the Danes who dressed themselves to look like men, and devoted almost every instant of their lives to the pursuit of war . . . for they abhorred all dainty living, and used to harden their minds and bodies with toil and endurance. They put away all the softness and lightmindedness of women, and inured their womanish spirit to masculine ruthless-

This twelfth-century illustration depicts the invasion of England by Viking warriors in 866.
(Courtesy of Art Resource.)

ness. . . . They devoted those hands to the lance which they should rather have applied to the loom. They assailed men with their spears whom they could have melted with their looks, they thought of death and not of dalliance."

Saxo's story tells that King Siward had two sons, Wemund and Osten, and a daughter, Alfhild, "who showed almost from her cradle such faithfulness to modesty, that she continually kept her face muffled in her robe." Her father gave her "a viper and a snake to rear" to ensure her "close keeping." Anyone seeking to get near the princess would have formidable gatekeepers to overcome.

Alf, son of King Sigar of Denmark, whose hair had such a "wonderful dazzling glow that his locks seemed to shine silvery," offered himself as a suitor to Princess Alfhild. Siward's answer to Alf's appeal was "that he would accept that man for his daughter's husband of whom she made a free and decided choice."

But Alfhild's mother was "stiff against the wooer's suit." She spoke to her daughter privately. Though Alfhild "warmly praised her suitor for his valour" and was "captivated by charming looks," her mother soon turned her against the young man: "Thus Alfhild was led to despise the young Dane; whereupon she exchanged woman's attire for man's attire and, no longer the most modest of maidens, began the life of a warlike rover."

Having spurned her suitor, the princess recruited a crew of "many maidens who were of the same mind" and embarked on a career of sea roving. These like-minded maidens, attired as men, could have been her companions, or may have come from the lower classes. In any case, they must have been a tough, muscular bunch because the longboats relied more on oars than sails for propulsion. Fighting with hand-to-hand weapons required enormous physical strength and stamina.

Perhaps the women had learned their seafaring skills on fishing vessels in the absence of men. They had probably experienced killing by butchering farm animals, which was a common chore for medieval women.

After several expeditions, the women pirates "happened to come to a spot where a band of rovers were lamenting the death of their captain who had been lost in war." Apparently, the male pirates were so taken by Alfhild's charm and agreeable manner that they asked her to join forces with them and be their captain. She agreed and "did deeds beyond the valour of woman." For months, the now-coed pirate crew, under the command of Alfhild, plundered up and down the Danish coast, terrorizing vessels.

Since subduing pirates was an important part of regal business, King Sigar sent the young crown prince of Denmark, Alfhild's rejected suitor, to conquer the treacherous robbers. Alf made "many toilsome voyages" in pursuit of the raiders. Finally, the Danes "crossed the frozen waters" and sailed to Finland. Upon entering a narrow gulf, they sent some men to reconnoiter and learned that the harbor was being held by a few ships—Alfhild had already sailed her fleet into the same narrows.

This image of the Viking princess Alfhild was made centuries after her death. (Courtesy of North Wind Picture Archive.)

Seeing strange ships in the distance, the pirate captain, dressed for combat in armor and helmet, commanded her crew to row swiftly to meet them. The plan was to attack the foe before being attacked. Alf's men tried to persuade him against engaging in battle, but he would not be swayed, and soon a fierce sea battle was underway in the Gulf of Finland. Although Alfhild's pirates had been equal to the defenses of the poor coastal towns, they were no match for the well-trained royal navy. The sailors swarmed over the pirates, killing most of the crew.

When the sea battle began, Prince Alf "leapt on Alfhild's prow, and advanced toward the stern, slaughtering all that withstood him." His comrade, Borgar, ripped the helmet from the captain's head and Alf, "seeing the smoothness of her chin, saw that he must fight with kisses and not with arms; that the cruel spears must be put away, and the enemy handled with gentler dealings."

Standing before Alf was his adversary, "the woman whom he had sought over land and sea in the face of so many dangers." Rejoicing that he had finally found Alfhild, he proposed marriage.

According to Saxo, Alf and Alfhild were married and had a daughter named Gurid. Apparently, Alfhild changed "her man's apparel to a woman's," gave up her career, and retired from the sea.

Borgar, a member of the royal navy, "wedded the attendant of Alfhild, Groa." Whatever happened to the other "maidens of the same mind" who survived the

This engraving depicts Alfhild battling Prince Alf.

bloody battle is not recorded in the chronicle. We can only speculate as to whether they carried on their ruthless and roving ways of living.

Years later, the Viking surge of piracy dwindled. Christianity was consolidated in Denmark around 1000, in Norway fifty years later, and in Sweden almost one hundred years after that. The end of the Viking era was followed by several centuries barren of major piratical activity.

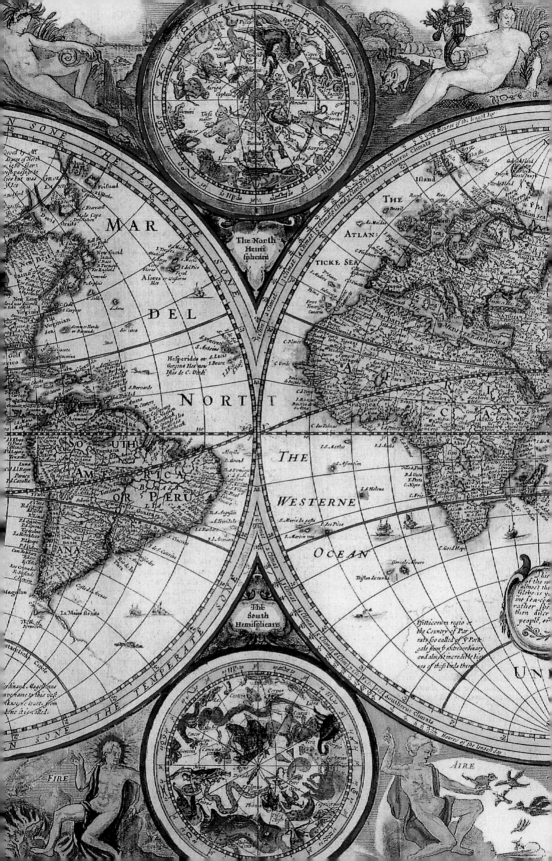

GRACE O'MALLEY

Irish Pirate Queen

Stories of notorious pirate Grace O'Malley, known in Ireland as "Granuaile," abound. Her sixteenth-century exploits spanned fifty years and extended from Scotland to Spain. Her history has gathered legends like barnacles. A tomb on Clare Island holds a skull reputed to be hers. Tradition states that a curse protects it from thieves.

Though her history lives somewhere in the fog of legend, Grace O'Malley, "the great spoiler and chief commander and director of thieves and murderers at sea," spent her time on Earth in a remote region of Ireland. Official state dispatches from the age of Queen Elizabeth contain accounts of her deeds.

Grace O'Malley, the "Pirate Queen," belonged to a century of "exploration and discovery, of wars and

Queen Elizabeth's reign was marked by extensive exploration and England's development as a world power. (National Portrait Gallery, London)

intrigue, of armadas and invasions, of glorious empires at the pinnacle." Hers was the age of Henry VII, Elizabeth I, Philip of Spain, Francis Drake, Walter Raleigh, and William Shakespeare.

Born in the early part of the sixteenth century, Grace was the only daughter of Dudara and Margaret O'Malley. Dudara (meaning Black Oak) ruled Umhall, the country around island-strewn Clew Bay, well known for its dangerous reefs and currents.

The daring, seagoing O'Malley clan differed from the majority of Irish clans in that the primary source of their income came from the sea. They sailed as far afield

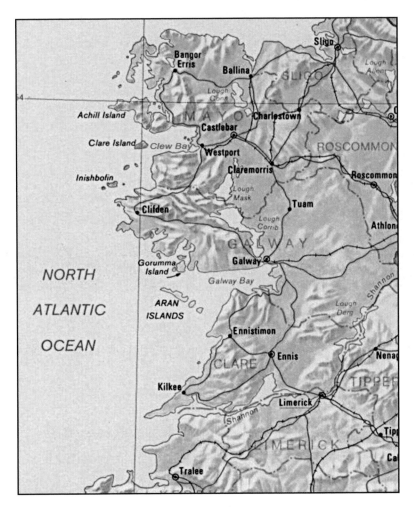

The region of Connaught, in northwest Ireland, where the O'Malleys lived.

as Spain, Scotland, and Brittany in their agile galleys powered by oar and sail. They sold salted fish, beef hides, tallow, and woolens in lucrative markets abroad.

The O'Malleys and their neighboring clans paid little attention to the affairs of the country. Independent chieftains ruled each state, spending their resources and energies on constant petty warfare and survival. Be-

A modern-day view of Clew Bay, looking out at Clare Island.

cause of the O'Malleys' remote habitat, young Grace grew up in a period of relative freedom from outside powers.

Much of Grace's childhood is the subject of folklore. One legend describes an incident that occurred in her early years on Clare Island. A brood of eagles had been carrying off the O'Malleys' sheep, taking them to their nests high on a cliff. Grace decided to end this nuisance herself by climbing the cliff to the nest and slaughtering the birds. Supposedly, the talons of the angry eagles gashed her forehead, leaving deep scars that never disappeared.

Grace's early childhood revolved around the family homes at Belclare and Clare Island. The O'Malleys, like other Irish families, established and maintained monasteries and abbeys on their lands. The abbey at Murrisk was near the O'Malley home at Belclare. Nestled around the outskirts of the O'Malleys' sphinx-like fortress were the thatched mud-and-stone cabins of the clan. In front stretched the sea. The clan's herds of cattle and sheep grazed on the hillsides.

Traveling bards entertained the chieftain's household in the winter. These poets and musicians also provided news and gossip from other parts of the country. Favorite pastimes included gambling and card playing.

In the summer, Grace's father moved his household to a "booley," a temporary summer dwelling in the uplands where the cattle herds could graze. These structures lacked the basic comforts of the permanent home. While "booleying," Dudara continued to fish and trade, unlike land-bound chieftains.

Grace's mother, Margaret, managed the household and served as hostess to the clan gatherings. Margaret supervised the work of the women—spinning, weaving, and dyeing clothes, churning butter, preparing the meals, and maintaining the residences.

Since the fifth century, when Christianity reached Ireland, a woman's place was in the home. Women's names appeared in historical records of the day only if they were the wives of chieftains. From an early age, Grace's interests lay not in her mother's domain but in her father's world of ships, trade, politics, and power.

Dudara O'Malley was a "swarthy, broad-shouldered chieftain, of great physical strength, his fair hair falling to his shoulders and cut in the traditional 'glib' or fringe across his forehead." He wore the chieftain's cloak, fastened with a gold pin and falling in folds to the ground. In his belt he carried a "Skeyne" or knife.

Perhaps her father's character and even physical attributes caused Grace to emulate him, to dress like him, to adopt his lifestyle—and to become more like a son than a daughter. No doubt her early years spent on the edge of the ocean instilled a love for the maritime that lasted throughout her life.

A legend explains Granuaile's nickname, "Grainne Mhaol" (meaning bald). As a young child, she pleaded to sail to Spain with her father. When her mother reminded Grace that a sailor's lot was no life for a young lady, Grace promptly cut off her long locks to look like the boys who sailed. Grace was allowed to go with her father, sailing to Spain and Portugal. She became an expert warrior, both on land and at sea.

When she was fifteen, Grace's father arranged for her to marry a local chieftain, Donal O'Flaherty, linking two of the most prominent seafaring families in western Ireland. She began her new life at Bunowen, her husband's tower-house fortress, located beside a concealed inlet.

Mystery shrouds much of Grace's life as the wife of the reckless and aggressive Donal. The marriage produced two sons and a daughter. In the beginning, Grace seemed to conform to expectations, assuming her duties as mistress of two castles.

Donal O'Flaherty, however, proved to be irresponsible, and his clansmen turned to his wife for help. Grace emerged as leader of the O'Flaherty clan. This began her life as a pirate.

Lumbering merchant ships on their way to Galway were prime targets for Grace and her men. Swooping out from the cover of islands in swift galleys, the pirates forced the ships to halt. Scrambling aboard, they pillaged and plundered. Laden with loot, Grace and her men disappeared into the mists and safety of Bunowen.

Local officials were powerless against such attacks, and the English did not have the ships or sufficient knowledge of the country and its remote coastline to apprehend Granuaile. Cartography was still being developed during the reign of Elizabeth, and Clew Bay was unknown territory.

Grace also took control of the clan's trading expeditions. She sailed to Munster, Scotland, Spain, and Portugal.

According to legend, Grace's husband died while trying to seize control of an island fortress known as Cock's Castle. After his death, the Joyces, longtime enemies of the O'Flahertys, took the castle. With Donal dead, the Joyces were confident that the castle belonged to them. But the joy in the Joyces' camp ended abruptly when Grace led the O'Flahertys in a surprise attack and regained the castle. She demonstrated such skill and heroism that the castle was renamed Hen's Castle.

Later, when this island fortress was under siege again, Grace ordered her men to strip the lead roof off the castle and melt it down. The molten liquid tumbled over the

The ruins of Hen's Castle. (National Library of Ireland)

turrets onto the soldiers below, who quickly retreated.

Although Grace proved to be a successful leader, Irish law did not allow a woman chieftain. Following the death of her husband, she returned to her father's domain on Clare Island, taking with her a band of two hundred men. She commanded the O'Malley fleets on errands of trade and piracy in what she described as "maintenance by land and sea"—earning both a fortune and a reputation as a fearless sea captain.

For over half a century, she led her men, contrary to the conventions of the time. Undoubtedly, her accomplishments contributed to her men's loyalty. "Outenduring and outdoing her men," she forged a lasting bond.

Grace had to possess expert knowledge of navigation, the dangerous coastline, her ships, and the elements to survive on the wild Atlantic. Conditions onboard a ship in the sixteenth century were crude: "Skin toughened under the barrage of wind and salt spray, hands and nails were hardened and split by hawser and canvas, bare feet became chafed from the rough swaying boards, sodden woolen trews and linen shirts itched, cold food lodged, undigested."

Eventually, international events affected Grace's maritime operations. Relations between England and Ireland had long been tense as the Irish struggled against oppressive and unwelcome English rule. England was now on the brink of war with Spain and worried that the Catholic nation would find sympathizers in Catholic Ireland, who would agree to harbor Spanish ships. The English government pushed westward into remote areas such as Mayo. Realizing that she needed a more secure base for her ships and crews than Clare Island, Grace decided to remarry. She did the choosing this time, basing her decision on the castle rather than its owner.

Grace married Richard-in-Iron Bourke, who owned Rockfleet Castle on the north shore of Clew Bay. The marriage was for "one year certain," and if after that period either party wished to withdraw, they were free to do so. One year later, Bourke returned from one of his warring missions to find Rockfleet Castle locked against him. Grace shouted from the ramparts of the castle, "I dismiss you," meaning she was divorcing him. She informed him that his castle was now hers. But Grace and

An eighteenth-century representation of Grace O'Malley's castle at Rockfleet.

Richard eventually reunited and lived together at Rockfleet Castle.

Their son, Theobald, was born around 1567. Records show his name as Tibbot-na-Long or "Theobald of the ships." According to legend, he was born on the high seas. The day after his birth, Turkish pirates attacked Grace's ship. As the battle raged on deck, her captain came below where Grace lay with her newborn son. He pleaded for help. She lambasted him: "May you be seven-times worse this day twelve months, who cannot do without me for one day." The new mother stormed onto the deck. The Turks, distracted by this disheveled female apparition, stood transfixed while Grace led her men to victory.

In 1576, Sir Henry Sidney, the first English deputy sent into western Ireland, met "the most famous feminine sea captain, Grany I Mallye." Why Grace risked capture by requesting a meeting with Sidney is open to speculation. Perhaps she realized that she could not survive without good relations with the English. Grace pledged loyalty to Sidney. But in so doing she gave her promise "a broad interpretation and continued as before, a scourge of the sea, taking tolls and raiding and pirating the ships that ventured within her domain." On a plundering expedition in 1577, Grace was captured and imprisoned in Dublin Castle for eighteen months.

Her husband Richard died in 1583. This time, Grace stayed in her marital home. She had ample livestock and plenty of supporters. She was now fifty-three years old and seemed ready to carry on as before—but it was not to be.

As hostility between England and Spain intensified, the English governor of Ireland, Richard Bingham, took bold steps to try to control the island nation. Eventually, he captured Grace and "caused a new pair of gallows to be made for her last funeral." But the chieftains of Mayo obtained her release by submitting hostages.

Bingham retaliated by taking Tibbot-na-Long hostage in an attempt to ensure Grace's good behavior. He also confiscated her enormous cattle herds. Her oldest son, Owen O'Flaherty, died while in the custody of Bingham's brother, and her second son, Murrough, incurred his mother's anger by siding with Bingham. To punish Murrough, she "manned out her navy of galleys, landed in Ballinahinche where he dwelleth, burned his town and spoiled his people of their cattle and goods and murdered 4 of his men who made resistence." Then she sailed for Clew Bay, her ships laden with the spoils of the attack.

In 1592, Bingham seized part of her fleet. Time was running out, as even the outlying areas of Ireland came under the English net. A new map of the country depicting the remote havens of Ireland was issued. Grace's name appears on the map above the region that she controlled—the only woman ruler so recognized.

The next year, after Bingham imprisoned her son Tibbott-na-Long for treason, Grace appealed directly to the queen of England, Elizabeth I. Aware that the queen knew of her piracy, Grace related her version of events and requested her son's release from prison.

Intrigued by the petition, the queen dispatched eighteen "articles of interrogatory"—or questions—to be answered by Grace. Her deft replies provide an informative account of her life. She followed her correspondence to court, sailing her ship from Clew Bay to London for an audience with the queen.

Unfortunately, the details of the meeting of these two illustrious women have been lost. The two rulers, both in their declining years, must have been a study in contrasts: one a weather-beaten woman in somber Gaelic dress; the other with chalk-like features in a richly embroidered gown sewn with jewels.

During the conversation with Elizabeth, a powdered and coiffed lady-in-waiting, noticing that Grace needed a handkerchief, presented a cambric-and-lace one to her. After using it, Grace tossed it into the fire. Elizabeth informed her that the handkerchief was meant to be kept in her pocket. An astonished Grace replied that in Ireland they had a higher standard of cleanliness than to pocket a soiled article.

The "Pirate Queen" made such an impression on Elizabeth that she granted all of Grace's requests, going against the advice of Governor Richard Bingham. However, the queen underestimated the talents of this "aged

Grace O'Malley (left) *stands before Queen Elizabeth of England to negotiate the release of her son from an English prison.* (From the *Anthologia Hibernica*)

woman." Following her successful mission to London, Grace returned to her plundering ways, under the guise of fighting the queen's "quarrel with all the world." In 1597, at the age of sixty-six, she sailed as far as Scotland, continuing her trade of "maintenance by land and sea."

Mystery shrouds the death of Grace O'Malley. Historians believe she died about 1603 and was buried in the abbey on Clare Island, at the edge of the ocean that sustained her long and eventful life. Rockfleet Castle still stands today, a sentinel overlooking the quiet waters of Clew Bay. In the west of Ireland, pirate Grace O'Malley's stone fortresses are reminders of a commanding woman, "famous for her stoutness of courage and person, and for sundry exploits done by her at sea."

TIMELINE

1530   Grace O'Malley born in Umhall, County Mayo, Ireland.

1533   Elizabeth Tudor (later Elizabeth I) born.

1546   O'Malley marries to Donal O'Flaherty.

1558   Elizabeth I crowned queen of England.

1560   Donal O'Flaherty killed.

1564   William Shakespeare born.

1566   O'Malley marries Richard-in-Iron Bourke.

1577   O'Malley arrested and jailed for eighteen months.

1583   Richard-in-Iron dies.

1583   O'Malley's oldest son killed.

1588   The Spanish Armada defeated.

1593   O'Malley meets with Queen Elizabeth I.

1603   Grace O'Malley dies; Queen Elizabeth I dies.

LADY KILLIGREW

Pirate Magnate

Grace O'Malley was not the only famous female pirate of her time. When Elizabeth I ascended to the English throne in 1558, piracy was "so general as to be scarcely disreputable." Many people in authority in England dabbled in piracy. Not only did the crown receive a percentage of the loot but the nobility, the navy, civil servants, and custom officers in the harbors all profited. In 1563, over four hundred known pirates sailed the four seas that washed the coasts of England.

Elizabethan piracy was driven by a network of big pirate syndicates, elaborate systems of harbors of sale and harbors of refuge that dotted the countryside. The greatest of these pirate magnates were the Killigrews of Cornwall in the southwesternmost tip of England.

Cornwall, England, located on the southwesternmost tip of the British Isles, was an excellent home base for pirating activities. (Library of Congress)

Sir John Killigrew, vice admiral of Cornwall, inherited the flourishing pirate syndicate business from his father and uncle. Aided by his mother, Lady Killigrew, Sir John expanded the syndicate. Lady Killigrew had learned the trade from her father, Philip Wolverston, widely known as the Suffolk "gentleman pirate." She had helped her late husband into the business. Over the years, she successfully plied her trade, avoiding confrontations with the law. As a plunderer, Lady Killigrew was described as "leading attacks in the same way as Artemisia [a female pirate of ancient Greek] had—as a woman born to it." Historians present the Killigrews as

The counties of England.

"vultures preying on every ship that landed on their coast, their sense of entitlement the result of centuries of privilege."

The Killigrews ran a large efficient business. They controlled the coasts of Cornwall, Devon, Dorset, Wales, and South Ireland. Lady Killigrew and her son took an active part in the raids. They were by no means "above taking the boarding axe into their own hands."

The Killigrew enterprise purchased and chartered ships, bought provisions for the pirates, bribed officials, and took care of any additional expenses—and still raked in enormous profits. A pirate ship that had successfully raided a merchant ship had only to sail into Falmouth Harbor, a safe harbor owned by the Killigrews. The captain would report his arrival to the syndicate leader and supply him with a list of the articles of the booty. The syndicate would then arrange for the sale of the loot, taking four-fifths of the profits. The one-fifth share of the earnings may have been less than that earned by freelance pirates, but the Killigrew system offered regular work with no capital outlay or worries over sales, plus security from the law.

A popular and well-known refuge among pirates was the Killigrew home, Arwenack Castle. The castle was the "finest and most costly" in the county. Located close to the sea, Arwenack and its surrounding estate sprawled over a secluded section of Falmouth. Legend has it that a secret tunnel ran from Arwenack Castle to the harbor, through "which the pirates were able to bring the booty

The remains of the Killigrews' Arwenack Castle and Pendennis fort.

into the Killigrews' cellar vaults without being seen." Lady Killigrew provided food and drink for the pirate crews and entertained lavishly for the pirate captains at Arwenack Castle.

The only other building near Arwenack Castle was the fortress of Pendennis, built by King Henry VIII. Armed with one hundred cannon, the fortress could have been a serious threat to pirates. But because Sir John was the hereditary royal governor of the fortress—a high honor in England—the structure posed no danger to visiting pirate ships.

After Sir John was appointed president of the Commission of Piracy—a commission designed to end Cornwall piracy—it seemed that nothing, including Queen Elizabeth, could stop the Killigrew operation. The Killigrews enjoyed favor at court because of their kinship to the queen's principal minister, Sir William Cecil. Sir John's political influence protected him, although government officials knew that he engaged in piracy against English and foreign ships. Only once in a while were they unlucky enough to come across people with even better connections to the ruling class.

In 1571, William Somerset, Earl of Worcester, set out to cross the English Channel with a christening gift of a golden salver from Queen Elizabeth to the infant daughter of Charles IX of France. Pirates from the Killigrew clan attacked his ship. The earl managed to flee with the tray, leaving the robbers five hundred pounds in cash.

When she heard the news of the attack, the queen ordered a raid along the Channel coastal regions. Out of the hundreds of pirates arrested, only three were executed. In lieu of being brought to trial, many were pressed into the queen's navy. Elizabeth wanted to strengthen her navy in anticipation of war with Spain. With their battle experience, the crews of pirate ships were the best recruits available. The queen saw no reason to hang them when they could serve on men-of-war.

The Killigrews lost some men to the queen's navy, but not their business. Over the next ten years, they continued to prosper. Then, in early January 1582, Lady Killigrew looked out of her drawing room window to see a Spanish ship, the *Marie,* docked right in front of Arwenack Castle.

A fierce storm had driven the ship into Falmouth

Harbor on New Year's Day. The crew put up at the Penryn Inn to wait for the weather to pass. From the moment the ship dropped anchor, rumors abounded of the fabulous cargo—silks, spices, and a dozen or more barrels of Spanish doubloons—in her hold. The owners, Juan de Chavis and Captain Philip de Oryo, were not the least bit worried about the safety of their ship. After all, they had anchored right in front of the Killigrew castle, knowing that Sir John was in charge of combating the pirates.

At midnight on Sunday, January 7, 1582, a small boat slipped into the private landing place at Arwenack. Details of the incident differ, but the men in the boat, their breaths forming cold clouds in the night air, must have waited anxiously. It was pitch-black. Even though the storm had passed, the dark clouds as yet had not cleared. Suddenly, out of the secret tunnel leading from the great house on the hill emerged a tall, slender figure—Lady Killigrew. She stepped into the boat and gave the order to move off.

The men pulled at their oars as the dinghy glided through the inky black water toward the *Marie*. They pulled alongside the Spanish merchant ship, and ten black figures snaked up the dangling rope ladder. With all on deck, Lady Killigrew ordered her trusted house servants, Henry Kendall and John Hawkins, and the other pirates to silence the watch and attend to the crew asleep down below. Swinging their cutlasses, Lady Killigrew and her men went about their tasks, quickly throwing the bodies of the Spaniards overboard.

Lady Killigrew soon learned that Juan de Chavis and Captain Philip de Oryo were not on board the ship. Her plan had called for no survivors. Hawkins explained to his enraged mistress that no amount of persuasion could change the owners' minds about spending their last night in port at a tavern in Penryn.

Still upset over the turn of events, Lady Killigrew commanded the seven seamen to take the ship to Baltimore in Ireland and sell it and its contents. And if they were unable to find a buyer for the *Marie* in Ireland, their orders were to scuttle her. The tall figure silhouetted against the night sky emphasized that there were to be no reminders of this night, and should they not return with her share of the money, there would be dire consequences.

While Lady Killigrew instructed her pirates, Kendall and Hawkins brought up several large barrels from the hold and lowered them over the side of the ship into the dinghy. After assisting Lady Killigrew, the servants shoved the boat off from the *Marie* and rowed hard. Soon, they felt the ground scrape under the bottom of the boat. They moored the boat and carried the plunder up the secret tunnel to Arwenack. Lady Killigrew had informed her men that no one was to know about the attack—not even Sir John.

The next morning, Lady Killigrew directed the opening of the barrels. To her amazement, they contained

Opposite: *Pirates overtake a Spanish merchant ship in this evocative oil painting by Howard Pyle.* (Delaware Art Museum, Wilmington)

only leather, some Holland cloth—fine linen cloth from Holland—and a few pieces of eight. There were no doubloons. No jewels. No silks. No expensive spices. The stuff was not of much value to her, but to the ship's owners the pieces of cloth and scraps of leather were valuable evidence. She had to get rid of the contents of the barrels.

Since the Holland cloth was so commonplace that it could not be identified, Lady Killigrew parceled it out among the ladies of her household. Miffed that the contents were not of more value, Lady Killigrew kept not only her own share of the linen cloth but that of her personal maid servant as well. She placed the more easily identified leather in a cask and had it buried it in the garden at Arwenack.

In the meantime, Chavis and Oryo arrived at the harbor to set sail and found their ship gone. Immediately, they filed a formal complaint with the president of the Cornwall Commission of Piracy—headed by Sir John Killigrew.

After reading the cargo list of the missing ship, Sir John remembered that several bolts of Holland cloth and some new chairs had recently appeared at the Killigrew home. He questioned his mother but did not receive a satisfactory answer.

Kendall and Hawkins already had reputations for their dealings with pirates, so it came as no surprise when suspicion fell on them, but they had alibis ready. The two men said that on Sunday they had been drinking all night at the Penryn Inn. Innkeeper Elizabeth Bowden swore that they had been there from nine o'clock in the evening.

Though still suspicious of his mother, Sir John swayed the commission—most of whom were either members of the syndicate or close friends of the Killigrews—toward the verdict he preferred. Having found no evidence to implicate any known person, the Commission of Piracy ruled the act was piracy by a person or persons unknown.

But the commission underestimated Juan de Chavis and Philip de Oryo. The men suspected foul play and decided to seek justice by taking matters into their own hands. The commission, happy to see the Spaniards leave Cornwall, quickly approved their request for safe conduct to London. What the Commission of Piracy did not know was that Chavis and Oryo had connections at court.

Once in London, they contacted their friend the Earl of Bedford, a member of the Privy Council. These councilors, appointed by the queen, advised her on important matters. After listening to their story, the earl agreed that the commission's verdict was not sound.

When Queen Elizabeth heard of the attack, she was glad. For some time she had been waiting for the opportunity to break the Killigrews' power. Here, at last, was concrete evidence of murder and robbery and a chance to regain control of strategic Falmouth Harbor.

The Earl of Bedford ordered Sir Richard Grenville and Edmund Tremayne to investigate the matter. The first person they spoke to was Sir John's daughter. She implicated her grandmother when she admitted receiving a bolt of Holland cloth and two leather chairs from Kendall.

That evidence alone was not enough to convict a noble thief, but it did cause Elizabeth Bowden, the tavern keeper, to change her story. She suddenly recalled that Kendall and Hawkins had come to the inn well after midnight and not at nine as she had earlier testified.

Fearing the gallows, Kendall and Hawkins began to talk and tried to lay the blame on Lady Killigrew. The inquiry resulted in the arrest and trial of Kendall and Hawkins, as well as Lady Killigrew. Condemned to death, Hawkins and Kendall perished on the gallows. Lady Killigrew, also sentenced to die, received a reprieve from Queen Elizabeth, saving her from the hangman's noose at the last moment. She would linger in prison for years, though little is known about the rest of her life.

Reportedly, Kendall's last statement on the gallows was that he "lamented nothinge more than that they had not the company of that old Jesabel [traitor] Killigrew at that place as in justice we ought to, and I beg Almighty God that some remarkable judgment might befall her."

From that day forward, large, fancy balls and great banquets were no longer held at Arwenack. There was no more entertaining of nobility, no more pirates visiting the great house. Sir John squandered the Killigrew fortune gambling, then imposed impossible taxes on his tenant farmers. Desperate for cash, he cut a deal with the

Spaniards, promising to rent Falmouth Harbor to them as the starting point for an invasion of England. Before his scheme could be implemented, the Spanish Armada was soundly beaten by the English navy in 1588. Some say that he planned to double-cross the Spaniards once he received their money. Others contend that he was a traitor.

There are few records of the activities of the pirate syndicates in the last decade of the sixteenth century. However, in the spring of 1598, documents show that, sixteen years after Lady Killigrew plundered the *Marie,* authorities arrested and imprisoned Sir John Killigrew for his piratical and traitorous activities. With the breakup of the mighty Killigrew syndicate—which once reigned supreme on the entire western coast of England—piracy in the English Channel almost came to a standstill.

TIMELINE

1533   Elizabeth Tudor born.
1558   Elizabeth I ascends to the throne of England.
1588   The Spanish Armada defeated.
1598   Sir John Killigrew arrested and imprisoned for piracy.

MARIA COBHAM

"Dead Cats Don't Mew"

Pirating during the 1700s, Maria Cobham and her husband Eric followed a no-survivors policy. They held to an old pirate saying: "Dead cats don't mew."

Maria Lindsey was born in Plymouth, a bustling seaport in Devon, England. Plymouth was the home port of many famous adventurers. It was here in 1577 that Sir Francis Drake set out on his voyage around the world. In 1588, the English sailed from Plymouth to meet the enormous fleet of the Spanish Armada—one so large that eyewitnesses said "the ocean groaned under its weight."

Records reveal little about Maria's early life. She grew up in Plymouth, and it was there she met the man she would marry. One day as she walked down the main

A sixteenth-century depiction of the busy harbor at Plymouth, where young Maria Lindsey first met her future husband, Eric Cobham.

street, Maria noticed a dapper-looking sea captain. Dressed in fine clothes, he stood out among the throngs of sailors milling about the streets of Plymouth. After a few hours of conversation with Captain Eric Cobham in a quayside tavern, she went aboard his cutter. Maria listened as Cobham explained he had only recently turned pirate.

Eric Cobham was born in Poole, Dorsetshire. At the age of eighteen, he joined a smuggling gang, running brandy from France to England. To celebrate his twenty-first birthday, he crossed into France with a band of smugglers and loaded 10,000 gallons of brandy aboard his sloop. He slipped back across the English Channel without being apprehended.

But a little later on, as he cruised across from France—again with another heavy load of smuggled goods—an English cutter awaited him. The captured smugglers, including Cobham, spent two years in jail. Cobham told Maria that after his term at Newgate Prison, he joined a group of highwaymen. After a few months with the robbers, he abandoned them and traveled to Oxford, where he obtained a position as clerk at the Bradford House. The former smuggler found many opportunities to practice thievery in the hotel. One night, wandering around the hotel floors after midnight, he noticed a light under a third-floor door. Peeking through a crack, Cobham saw a man counting a pile of gold.

Cobham, barely getting by on the few shillings paid him by the owner of the inn, decided to take action. Watching surreptitiously up and down the hall, he tapped on the door of the room. The lodger opened the door cautiously, but Cobham pushed him aside and grabbed for the bag of gold.

During the struggle that followed, Cobham drew his knife, killed the lodger, and escaped with the gold. Later, he heard that the innkeeper had entered the same room an hour after Cobham's crime, found the guest dead, and was wrongly accused of the murder. The wealthy lodger, Mr. Hayes, came to Oxford to buy a substantial amount of property. The innkeeper knew of the gold and had made plans to murder Hayes.

After two weeks at Newgate Prison, the unfortunate innkeeper swung from the gallows for a crime he intended to commit but did not.

With four hundred pounds of gold, Cobham bought a new cutter at Bridgeport and mounted fourteen guns upon it. He had no trouble recruiting a crew from the docks. In eighteenth-century Britain, homeless families roamed the streets, and scrawny orphans begged on every corner. Many were glad to take up the life of a pirate. English rulers issued threats, bribes, and proclamations to end piracy, but with little success.

On his first cruise as a pirate, Cobham set off to plunder the North Sea. He soon sighted a ship from East India heading up the channel toward Bristol. He captured the vessel.

After overcoming the crew, the pirates forced the captain to reveal the whereabouts of his wealth. Cobham explained to Maria how he had persuaded the frightened captain to turn over his treasure—no less than 40,000 pounds in gold sovereigns, intended for the purchase of Chinese opium. Then, with this hoard in his possession, Cobham thrust his rapier through the captain's heart, sewed him up in a sack, and, with rocks for ballast, he dumped the body overboard.

Cobham instructed his pirates to carry out the same procedure with the other members of the captured crew. Maria, enchanted by the story, listened as Cobham described the scene: the terrible screams, yells of battle-crazed pirates, shrieks of the wounded. The deck was soon awash with blood. It took until midnight to complete the massacre. Then they stuffed the bodies in bags filled with rocks and tossed them overboard.

Having no use for the ship, the young captain scuttled the vessel. As he watched the beautiful ship disappear into the deeps, he relished his extraordinary luck. Then he sailed into Plymouth harbor where he met Maria.

Young Maria Lindsey, who apparently came from a good family, was not in the least disturbed by Cobham's cruelty. His adventures captivated her, and the couple married the next day. They took their honeymoon on his fourteen-gun cutter. Soon, more luckless sailors would be at the bottom of the ocean in canvas bags.

At first, having Maria on board caused some murmuring among the crew because they were not allowed women on their voyages. But Maria soon won the allegiance of the crew by using her influence with the captain to lighten their punishment when he imposed drastic penalties.

Maria was an apt pupil. She soon became as vicious a pirate as her husband, capturing and scuttling ship after ship.

When the pirates captured a craft with a young naval officer aboard, Maria liked his uniform so much that she had him stripped of his clothes in front of the other pirates. Then she ran him through with her sword. Shoving his body into a sack, she sewed him up and heaved him overboard. Maria wore the dead man's uniform from then on. She liked the outfit so much that she had replicas made and wore them both at sea and in port.

One day, while roaming the high seas, these daring sea bandits narrowly escaped capture by a British man-of-war. Fearing that Captain Cobham had been recognized, Maria suggested that they sail across the Atlantic to the New England coast. A month later, they sighted land—Nantucket Island.

The pirates went ashore at No Man's Land and liked it so much that they decided to spend the summer. Legend has it that Cobham buried 15,000 golden guineas on the island.

The island of Nantucket, located approximately twenty miles off Massachusetts's Cape Cod, was a prosperous whaling port and an appealing target and hideout for pirates of the Atlantic. (Library of Congress)

Later, after pillaging at Block Island, the Cobhams and their crew sailed for northern waters. There they lay in wait for vessels passing between Cape Breton and Prince Edward Island on route to Quebec from London. The pirates took money and merchandise from the captured vessels, killing the crews in the usual manner and scuttling the ships.

Maria always took an active part in the skirmishes. One day, using a recently stolen little dirk, she stabbed the captain of a Liverpool brig through the heart. Murder for her was a pleasure and a sport.

On another occasion, to indulge a whim, she insisted that a captain and his two mates be tied to a windlass. Then Maria went below. She came back on deck brandishing eight pistols. From a distance of twenty feet, she fired gun after gun until the last spark of life in the three men vanished. According to tradition, she never missed a shot.

For twenty years, the Cobhams sailed the high seas and amassed a fortune they hid in several English banks and buried on Atlantic islands. Finally, Captain Cobham grew weary of the life of butchery and scuttling ships. He wanted to settle down. Maria did not. But she finally agreed, on the condition that Cobham would buy Mapleton Hall, an elegant estate in Dorset, her husband's home port.

While Cobham went ashore to arrange for the purchase, Maria, for reasons unknown, took the crew out by herself. The next day, she overtook an East India merchant ship off Scotland. After a fierce encounter, she captured the vessel.

Taking the survivors aboard the cutter, Maria ordered the crew to put them in irons on the deck. Then she went into the galley and made a poisoned stew. Within an hour of eating the stew, all the prisoners were dead. Maria disposed of the bodies by throwing them overboard— no sacks and no sewing up this time—a villainous act as black as the flag under which she sailed.

She returned to Dorset and learned that her husband had not been able to buy the mansion at Mapleton after all. A short time later, Cobham did buy a large estate near Le Havre on the coast of France. It had its own snug little harbor. Here the retired pirates kept a pleasure yacht, employing some of the former crew as officers and sailors. Maria still wore her naval uniform and went on fishing expeditions.

The Cobhams began to raise a family. Within a period of five years, they produced two sons and a daughter, and Maria and her husband gave up piracy—almost.

One day while on a pleasure cruise, they encountered a big West Indian brig that lay becalmed just outside the bay. The couple decided to pay a social call on the captain of the merchant ship. Aboard the brig, they were enjoying the hospitality of their host when the temptations of former years became too strong. It took no more than eye contact between the couple to put a fiendish plan into action.

Maria invited the captain to board her yacht. Cobham

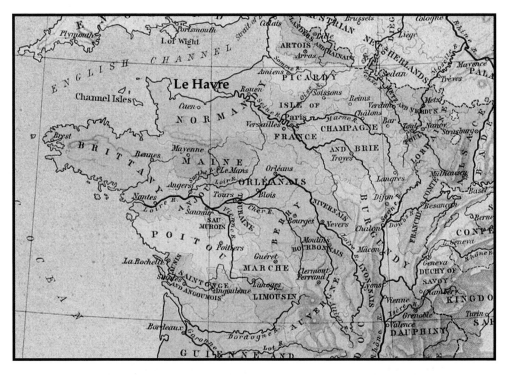

This map of northern France shows the port city of Le Havre in Normandy. The protected harbors and easy access to the English Channel made this an appealing home for the Cobhams.

whipped out a pistol and shot the captain through the head. Then they subdued the crew of the merchantman and disposed of the corpses in the usual manner—by sewing them up in gunnysacks and throwing them overboard.

Cobham sailed the prize into the harbor on their property. After altering the name of the brig, Maria and her husband took her to Bordeaux. They were able to sell her for a good price, no questions asked, adding still more to their riches. This deed turned out to be the last act of piracy for the Cobhams. They returned to the quiet of their estate.

Not long after, the Duc de Chartres visited Cobham and proposed that the ex-pirate take over the judgeship of the county courts. The magistrate had just died, and they were looking for an honest, reputable citizen to replace him. Stunned by the offer, Cobham wanted to decline, but Maria insisted that he accept. The aging pirate was now a judge. For the next twelve years, he found himself judging hundreds of cases. Ironically, this couple of blackguards not only escaped punishment for their crimes but also gained respectability. Judge Cobham became famous for his fairness and condemnation of wrongdoing.

But Maria did not adjust well to retirement. Possibly haunted by the specters of her grim past, she began to grow despondent. One day she told her husband that she needed some time alone to think. She went for a long walk along the towering cliffs and never returned.

Her husband found her cloak and scarf, along with an empty laudanum bottle, at the edge of a precipice. Two days later her body washed ashore. Laudanum had been Maria's favorite poison.

Maria's suicide left Judge Eric Cobham's conscience stricken. Although he never showed the slightest remorse before, he was now obsessed by the memory of the terrible deeds he had committed during his long period of crime at sea. He spent many hours at the local church in conference with the pastor.

Cobham lived to a ripe old age. Before he passed away, he called in the minister for his last confession. He revealed that during the last twelve years he had laboriously written out all the crimes that he and Maria committed during their many years of piracy. He made the pastor promise to publish the detailed confession after his death.

The published confession was an embarrassment to Cobham's socially prominent children and grandchildren. The descendants would have preferred to have the adventures of their wicked ancestors buried with them. Despite the family's efforts to buy the books up as rapidly as they appeared, the story of Maria Cobham, woman pirate of iniquity, survived.

TIMELINE

1533   Elizabeth Tudor born.
1558   Elizabeth I ascends the throne of England.
1577   Francis Drake sets out the circle the globe.
1588   The Spanish Armada is defeated by the English navy.

MARY READ

"Milord, we plead our bellies"

"**M**ilord, we plead our bellies." On Monday, November 28, 1720, in a jam-packed Jamaican courtroom, spectators erupted with laughter as two shackled pirates made their plea. The prisoners were not joking. They were indeed pregnant. In the eighteenth century, expectant mothers—no matter how guilty—escaped the hangman's noose because the law did not allow an unborn child to be killed.

One of the condemned women was Mary Read. She sailed the Caribbean beneath the black flag during the Golden Age of Piracy—the greatest era of piracy the world has ever known.

Published four years after the trial, a history of the "pyrates" includes the exploits of Mary Read and Anne Bonny, the only known women pirates of the Golden

English writer Daniel Defoe used the pseudonym of Captain Charles Johnson to publish his eighteenth-century history of pirates.

Age. The author of the 1724 best-seller *The General History of the Robberies and Murders of the Most Notorious Pyrates* was a mysterious Captain Charles Johnson—later determined to be Daniel Defoe, the author of *Robinson Crusoe*. He used trial transcripts, contemporary newspaper reports, and interviews to compile a detailed account of the two women's lives. According to one description, the story is "as strange a blend of fact and fiction . . . ever concocted." The author, anticipating this kind of reaction, acknowledged in the preface to the *History* that "it might be thought the story was no better than a novel or romance."

Mary Read's route to the Caribbean began in England. Her "young and airy" mother was pregnant when her sailor husband went to sea and never returned. In due time, she gave birth to a son.

Soon after, she discovered she was expecting a second child. Taking her infant son and her secret, she left the urban squalor of London to live in the country, where a tragedy not uncommon to the era struck. Her baby boy became ill and died. Mary, the illegitimate daughter, was born a few months later, near the end of the seventeenth century.

Life was harsh for a single woman with an illegitimate child. For four years, the two struggled to survive in the country. Finally, at her wit's end, Mrs. Read trudged back to London, hoping to receive help from her deceased husband's mother. Knowing that the grandmother disliked little girls, she planned to palm Mary off as her dead brother. Mrs. Read never reported her son's death or Mary's birth to the relatives. She trained Mary to talk and act like a boy and exchanged her girl's dress for a boy's breeches and coat.

The scheme worked, almost too well. The grandmother offered to let the "lad" and his mother live with her. Sensing the risks of such an arrangement, Mrs. Read declined but accepted a weekly allowance for their support. For many years, Mary maintained her false identify to keep the allowance.

Mary was thirteen when her grandmother passed away. The allowance stopped. The Reads were penniless again.

Mrs. Read solved the problem by hiring Mary—still dressed in boy's attire—out as a footboy to a French lady. Mary did not object to dressing as a boy. Being a boy gave her more freedom at a time when girls led extremely sheltered lives

Mary Read learned how to fight like a man during the War of the Spanish Succession. (National Maritime Museum, Greenwich, England)

But Mary's nature demanded more excitement than the dullness of blacking boots for a living. "Growing bold and strong, and having also a roving mind," she enlisted as a cabin boy on board a British warship. It was possible to get away with such a fraud since recruits had no medical examinations in the 1700s. Servicemen seldom bathed or washed the entire body. They habitually slept in their clothes. To pass as a man, a woman needed only to bind her upper body with a sash before donning a uniform.

Mary found the routine life of a seaman in the Royal Navy boring. After a short stint, she deserted and crossed the English Channel to Flanders (now Belgium and part of France). She joined a regiment of Flemish foot soldiers and served as a cadet during the War of the Spanish Succession. "She behaved herself with a great deal of Bravery" during the long marches, artillery barrages, and bayonet charges. Mary Read was fearless, daring, and ambitious. She hoped to earn a commission as an officer, but soon discovered that poor people did not rise through the ranks. Promotions were bought and sold.

Disappointed, Read transferred to a cavalry regiment. She loved riding into battle and won "the esteem of all her Officers." No one suspected that she was a girl.

One day a new man joined the troop and was assigned to her tent. When Read saw this handsome, strapping young soldier, she fell in love. Strange new emotions stirred within her as she galloped beside him in battle. She was in love with a man who didn't even know she was a woman. She became absentminded and neglected her military duties. Read insisted on accompanying her bunkmate wherever he went. Her odd behavior convinced her companions that Trooper Read had lost "his" mind.

Unable to contain her feelings any longer, Mary blurted out her secret. Astounded at first, the soldier soon recovered and asked her to marry him.

At the close of the campaign, Read and her former tent mate were married, to the delight of their comrades. The regiment paid for the wedding, including the bride's trousseau. For the first time in her life, Mary Read dressed as a woman—probably wearing fancy shoes, petticoats, and a low-cut silk dress.

As Defoe put it, "Two troopers, marrying each other, made a great noise." The newlyweds could not stay in the army. They received honorable discharges and, with contributions from the regiment, they opened the Three Horseshoes tavern, near Breda in Holland. Uniformed servicemen crowded the tavern every night. Mary seemed content in her role as a woman and a wife.

But like her mother, Mary was destined for a short married life. Her beloved husband died suddenly, bringing to an end the only domestic interlude in her life. Then she suffered a second blow—the return of peace that took away her English military customers. Brokenhearted, the impoverished widow gave up the empty inn, and her dress, for good.

Remembering the smell of gunpowder and the shouts of charging soldiers, Mary Read returned to her old life. She enlisted in an infantry regiment in Holland. But life in a peacetime garrison was far too dull for her. She left the army and signed on a Dutch merchantman bound for the Caribbean, hoping to find excitement in the New World—a decision that assured a name for her in history.

The island-studded Caribbean, with scalloped shores of countless inlets and cays, was the focus of intense pirate activity from 1492 until the nineteenth century. No ship was safe. Settlements along the Spanish Main (Spanish possessions along the coasts of Central and South America) did not escape the plundering.

During the centuries following Christopher Columbus, European nations jockeyed for control of the New

This colored chart depicts one of Sir Francis Drake's famed attacks on the Spanish Main at Santo Domingo, the capital of the island of Hispaniola. (National Maritime Museum, Greenwich, England)

World and its riches. The powers of Europe pitted their expansionist forces against one another in wars waged over the islands of the West Indies and the Spanish Main.

Pirates of every nationality, color, and creed preyed on silver- and gold-laden galleons, merchant ships, and slavers. Despite the religious antagonisms and alliances that divided their countrymen, pirate crews varied in their ethnic and religious makeup. These multicultural seafarers would play leading roles in three centuries of geopolitical drama.

Today, the term buccaneer is used loosely to refer to lawless adventurers on the high seas. The original buccaneers were French political and religious refugees who roamed the island of Hispaniola, which is now Haiti and the Dominican Republic. The buccaneers, with a burning hatred for anything Spanish, lived off the land with the sky as their roof. Their name came from their custom of smoking meat on *boucans*—French for wooden grills. They were sea robbers, swooping out from the many narrow channels and creeks to prey upon unsuspecting merchant ships.

The New World's mineral wealth also attracted Protestant Dutch *Zee Rovers* (Sea Rovers). The English called them freebooters. No matter what they called themselves, the Spanish government regarded foreign seamen as *piratas,* hated interlopers.

For thirty-three years during the Golden Age of Piracy—between 1692 and 1725—pirate raiders terrorized the sea lanes and disrupted trade. They ran their vessels as the buccaneers had done before them, electing their own captains and signing a set of articles, or rules, before setting sail.

By the late 1690s, British colonies along the Atlantic coast from Massachusetts to the Carolinas were welcoming the sea rovers in protest of the English monopoly on manufactured goods, as well as unfair prices. All the leading colonial seaports—New York, Boston, Philadelphia, Charleston—did business with the pirates.

Rebellious seafarers of that era signed aboard pirate vessels, lured by stories of vast treasures taken in forays. Often, the life of a pirate was chosen for reasons other than mere desire for wealth. Many sailors turned outlaw to live a life of freedom. They wanted to escape an

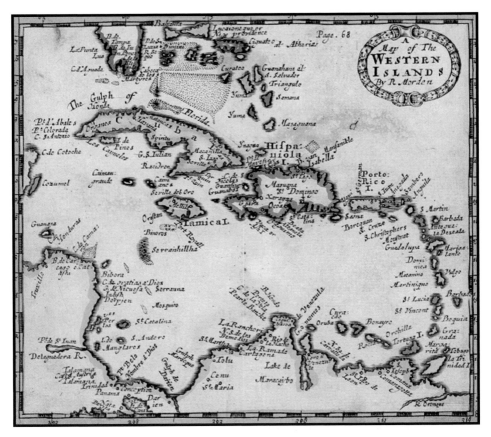

The islands of the Caribbean, where Mary Read gained notoriety during the Golden Age of Piracy.

oppressive caste system that permitted liberty only to the wealthy and well born. This is what Mary Read hoped to do.

Before reaching the Caribbean, the Dutch vessel on which Read sailed came under attack by English pirates from New Providence, a Bahamian haven for pirates. This was Mary Read's first encounter with pirates. The captain forced her, the only "Englishman" on board, to join the marauders. After plunder-

Mary Read reveals that she is a woman to a man she has fatally wounded in a duel. (National Maritime Museum, Greenwich, England)

ing the vessel, the pirates allowed the ship to continue on her journey.

Read, eager to live life to its fullest, did not hesitate when the captain growled for her to make her mark and join the pirates. By signing the ship's articles, she agreed to go "on the account," as the eighteenth-century pirates called it—meaning "No Prey, No Pay."

For a time, she sailed with the pirates, seeing plenty of action and expertly wielding her cutlass and pistol. Life aboard a pirate ship meant moments of intense excitement and terrifying danger when seizing a prize. After capturing a ship, the pirates beached their own in a secluded bay or cove to divide the treasure and celebrate.

A favorite pastime of the pirates was to hold a mock trial with buffoonish ceremony. Each pirate had a chance to play judge and prisoner. Music played an important part in pirate life, particularly songs sung in rhythm to work—chanteys and bawdy ballads, accompanied by fiddles, oboes, and recorders.

As a member of the pirate crew, Mary would have been expected to help with the repairing of spars, sails, rigging, and with careening. At regular intervals, it was necessary to careen the ship in order to maintain speed and maneuverability. Careening involved tilting the ship to one side and scraping off the weed and shell-encrusted bottom, and putting on an anti-fouling layer.

She likely went in search of food and fresh water to restock the ship. The erratic diet of pirates included sea turtles, goats, monkeys, and snakes, some of which they salted for future use. Europeans generally disliked the vegetables in use by the natives of the West Indian islands.

Mariners preferred beer or wine since water on board ship quickly became undrinkable. They seldom used forks. Most pirates ate with their fingers. One source describes their table manners: "They eat in a very disorderly manner more like a kennel of hounds." Meals were eaten in the cramped sleeping quarters filled with the smell of food, vermin, and excess cargo.

In 1718, Woodes Rogers, governor of the Bahamas, offered all pirates a royal pardon if they would abandon their ways. The record shows that Read and her ship-mates voluntarily surrendered and lived quietly ashore, "with the fruits of their adventures," on an island some distance from New Providence.

Read soon missed the free-roving ways of a pirate. When her money ran out, she packed her gear and headed back to sea. Along with several other ex-pirates, she went to New Providence and enlisted aboard a privateer, an armed vessel licensed to attack and seize the vessels of an enemy nation. Mary Read had government approval to sail against the Spaniards.

As soon as the ship left dock and New Providence disappeared below the blue horizon, the crew mutinied, took control of the vessel, and ran up the black flag. And so began Mary Read's association with Jack

Rackam and Anne Bonny. She never left pirating again.

In 1720, she would find herself kneeling alongside her friend Anne, both of them pregnant and begging for their lives.

TIMELINE

1660   Daniel Defoe is born.

1689   William III and Mary II crowned king and queen of England.

1701   The War of the Spanish Succession begins.

1702   Queen Anne succeeds to the throne.

1714   George I inherits the throne; the War of the Spanish Succession ends.

1719   *Robinson Crusoe* is published.

1724   Daniel Defoe, writing as Captain Charles Johnson, publishes *The General History of the Robberies and Murders of the Most Notorious Pyrates.*

1720   Mary Read and Anne Bonny are arrested and tried.

1721   Mary Read dies and is buried on April 28.

1731   Daniel Defoe dies.

ANNE BONNY

"A Fierce and Couragious Temper"

The other woman on trial that balmy day in November 1720 was Anne Bonny. The judge, Sir Nicholas Lawes, his floppy gray judicial wig askew, pronounced Anne Bonny, partner of Mary Read, an outlaw "confirmed in all wicked practices—a lusting, thieving, oathing female, best made use of on the gallows!" The mob listening outside the Admiralty Court at St. Jago de la Vega, Jamaica, jeered.

This was not Bonny's first trial. The previous time she was charged, her spectacular beauty had saved her. Jamaican court records show that the judge declared, "A more delectable doxie I have never seen—nor, for that matter, a more brazen one." She received a light sentence: threat of a flogging if she did not behave.

Like Mary Read, Anne Bonny was the product of a

Although the city of Port Royal, Jamaica, had once been known as a pirate safe haven, the city became a place of pirate execution during the 1700s after the passage of several strict antipiracy laws. (Library of Congress)

complicated family situation. She was born in Cork, Ireland, around 1700, the illegitimate child of a prominent lawyer, William Cormac, and Peg Brennan, the family maid. Cormac's wife left him, and the scandal affected his law practice. He decided to leave Ireland forever and start a new life in North America. Taking his mistress and their child, he settled in Charleston, South Carolina—a booming seaport then known as Charles Towne.

Cormac prospered in the new land. Not only was he in great demand as an attorney, he engaged in trading and soon became a wealthy plantation owner. His daughter Anne developed into a spunky, strong-willed young woman, with her own room, her own horses, and her own dogs, spending her time as she saw fit. She dressed in the finest materials and received an education from the best tutors.

Anne was about fifteen when her mother died. The young girl with "a fierce and couragious Temper" took over her father's household. She soon earned a fearsome reputation when, during a fit of passion that matched her flaming red hair, she killed a serving girl with a knife. She allegedly responded to the advances of a suitor by attacking him with such ferocity that he remained bed-ridden for several weeks.

Anne accompanied her father on trading trips to waterfront offices, warehouses, and the teeming docks of Charleston. Bawdy songs and shouts wafted through the air from the rowdy waterfront taverns. Pirate ships brought in much of the merchandise: cotton, sugar, spices, indigo, dyewoods, and silks. Her father probably did business with pirates.

Despite her growing reputation as a spitfire, Anne had many suitors. She spurned them all and married, without informing her father, a penniless seaman named James Bonny.

With his plans for marrying Anne to a prosperous Carolina merchant dashed, Cormac "turned her out of Doors." James Bonny, disappointed at seeing a fortune escape him, whisked his bride off to the pirates' nest on the island of New Providence.

In the early eighteenth century, the stench from Nassau—roasting meat, smoke, unwashed bodies, def-ecation, and rotting garbage stewing together under the broiling sun—filled the air long before the island came into view. Pirate sloops and captured merchant ships crowded the shimmering blue waters of the harbor. Abandoned prizes lay rotting on the beach, their ribs stripped as bare as skeletons. Ragged and dirty tents, improvised from discarded sails, fluttered in the trade winds like hundreds of unmade beds. Shacks of driftwood thatched with palm fronds littered the edge of the woods. The forest rustled and the water lapped against the wharves and in and out of tiny caves along the beach.

Life in the shantytown was chaotic. Women prepared food around open campfires as youngsters toddled amid the filth. Babies cried. Dogs yelped. Parrots shrieked obscenities. Singing and shouting echoed along the waterfront. Pirates stumbled from tavern to tavern, day and night.

To this pirate enclave—a mixture of squalor and natural splendor—came Anne and her sailor husband. Anne soon lost interest in Bonny. She reacted with disgust when he turned informer for Governor Woodes Rogers, who had been commissioned by the British government to stamp out piracy. She began looking elsewhere for companionship.

The rich silks and golden trinkets in the market dazzled Anne, as did the bronze-faced, bearded, swaggering pirates along the waterfront. She frequented the harborside taverns, often seeking the company of swashbuckling pirate captains such as Charles Vane, Blackbeard, and Ben Hornigold.

Then she met the bold and reckless Captain John Rackam. His fondness for splashy waistcoats, bright

The flamboyant pirate "Calico Jack" Rackam is remembered primarily for having the two famous women pirates, Mary Read and Anne Bonny, in his crew. (Courtesy of the Granger Collection.)

ribbons, and gaudy calico breeches earned him the nickname "Calico Jack." Rackam came into Nassau to claim the king's pardon and to receive a privateering commission. The dashing pirate captain offered an answer to Anne Bonny's yearning for a life at sea.

Calico Jack lavished on Anne flashy baubles from his booty. He even tried to buy her from her husband. Divorce by sale was an accepted practice at that time. But James Bonny refused the offer. He complained to Governor Rogers, who ordered Anne to return to her husband. Anne defied the order and ran away with Rackam.

That Rackam had no ship at this time only added to the bold adventure. Anne slipped aboard a sloop anchored in Nassau harbor and gathered information while Calico Jack rounded up a handful of his old cronies. On a rainy night, the gang swarmed over the gunwales of the vessel with Anne in the lead. Wearing an ordinary seaman's garb and carrying a sword in one hand and a pistol in the other, Anne surprised the two men on watch. She whispered to them that she would blow out their brains if they resisted. They did not resist.

The pirates cast off from the ship's moorings in the dark of night. The sloop glided silently out of the harbor. Down came the British flag. Up went the black flag. Anne Bonny and Calico Jack Rackam sailed off into the blue waters of the Bahamas and onto the pages of history.

The pirates cruised the Caribbean, taking and pillaging a number of small prizes, and even raiding some shore installations. Anne, dressed in men's clothing, fought and plundered with ruthless brutality. She wielded a cutlass with the best of the crew until she went ashore in Cuba to have a baby. After the delivery, she rejoined Rackam, apparently abandoning the child.

A year later, the king ordered a new amnesty. Calico Jack decided to take this one. He went to New Providence and took the pardon, promising never to resort to piracy again. He signed aboard an honest privateer. Anne, disguised as a man, accompanied him. Only a few days out of port, the crew mutinied. Rackam and Anne were the ringleaders.

Aboard the privateer-turned-pirate ship was a handsome, clean-cut young man who caught the roving eye of Anne Bonny. Anne admired the sailor's skill and daring. The shipboard friendship became a strong attraction, especially for Anne. She decided to reveal her identity, only to discover that the object of her desire was hiding the same secret. "He" was not a man, but Englishwoman Mary Read, who passed as an ordinary sailor. Each agreed to keep the other's secret.

In the weeks that followed, Anne Bonny and Mary Read fought side by side: "None among Rackam's crew were more resolute or ready to Board or undertake any Thing that was hazardous as Mary Read and Anne Bonny."

Calico Jack, disturbed by Anne's interest in the young sailor, threatened to cut his rival's throat. To dispel Rackam's jealous rage, Read let him in on the secret.

For some months, Rackam and his crew cruised the Caribbean, taking and looting merchant ships homeward bound from Jamaica. Forced to join the pirates in one of these successful raids was a handsome navigator with engaging manners.

Read fell in love with the young captive. She wasted

Mary Read, dressed as a man, slays her husband's rival in a duel. (Library of Congress)

no time in telling him that she was a woman. He returned her love, promising they would wed at the end of the voyage. Read agreed to what she later termed "as good a marriage in conscience as if it had been done by a minister in a church."

During the cruise, Read demonstrated her affection in one of the "most generous Actions that ever Love inspired." Following a quarrel with a hulking brute of a pirate, Read's husband was challenged to a duel. Fearing that the navigator—who was not an experienced fighter—would be killed, Read deliberately provoked an argument with the same man and challenged him to a duel herself.

Dueling was the accepted manner of settling disputes among pirates and conformed to a distinctive code. The participants went ashore to battle with cutlass and pistol until there was only one survivor.

Read and her opponent both missed on the exchange of pistol shots. A long and bloody contest with cutlasses followed. The duel ended with Read running the man through the body, wounding him mortally. Just as the ruffian crumpled in the sand, the navigator arrived for his duel—to find Mary Read standing over the dead pirate.

By midsummer 1720, Nassau was no longer a base for the outlaw pirate nation. British fortifications defended the land. Ex-pirates, who now sailed under the British flag, protected the sea. Most of the pirates of the West Indies abandoned their old haunts. Only a few diehard brigands continued to follow the trade in the Caribbean. One of that dwindling number was Calico Jack and his crew, including Mary Read and Anne Bonny. But their days were numbered.

In late September, Rackam and his crew paid a call at Harbor Island. They captured fishing vessels, taking provisions and gear. Then they landed on Hispaniola, where they slaughtered cattle to replenish their supplies.

By October, Rackam was operating off the north coast of Jamaica. He captured a schooner and one or two small trading vessels. Coasting the island in this manner proved to be Calico Jack's downfall.

Word reached the governor of Jamaica in November 1720 that Rackam lay anchored just off Negril Point on

the western end of the island. Bounty hunter Captain Jonathan Barnet set sail in a heavily armored privateer, hoping to capture the unrelenting pirate.

The navy sloop surprised the tipsy pirates at ten o'clock at night. As Rackam's big guns boomed, Captain

The legend of the fierce women pirates Anne Bonny (opposite) and Mary Read (above) began shortly after their deaths. This English engraving of them was made in 1724. (Courtesy of the Granger Collection.)

Barnet's men fired their arms across the narrow space of water between the two ships and threw grappling hooks over the pirate ship's gunwales, lashing the two vessels together. Sailors stormed aboard.

In the skirmish, all the pirates, including the once-daring Captain Rackam, fled below deck—except for Anne Bonny, Mary Read, and one other crew member. They remained topside to defend the ship. Howling like banshees, the two women flew at the sailors, firing their pistols and swinging their cutlasses.

Read drew two loaded pistols and screamed at the cowards below deck to "come up and fight like men." There was no answer. Realizing all was lost, she raised the hatch cover and turned both of her pistols into the hold. She pulled the triggers, killing one of the cowering pirates and wounding several others.

A moment later, the women, outnumbered, lost the battle. The sailors slapped the surviving pirates in chains and took them to St. Jago de la Vega (now Spanish Town), Jamaica to stand trial. After a brief imprisonment, they came before the Admiralty Court. Most of the men were tried on Wednesday, November 16, 1720. At the trial, Mary Read's young lover and several others claimed they served as pirates against their wills. They were set free.

Defoe's book on the pirates includes a frequently quoted statement that is absent from the court transcript. Read, when asked why she would risk public execution for the sake of pirating, supposedly replied

that to hanging, she thought it no great hardship, for, were it not for that, every cowardly fellow would turn

Pirate, and so infest the seas that men of courage must starve; that if it was put to the choice of the pirates, they would not have the punishment less than death, the fear of which kept some dastardly rogues honest; and that . . . the ocean would be crowded with rogues, like the land, and no merchant would venture out; so that the trade in a little time would not be worth following.

Defoe claims that Read commended the court for having acquitted her husband and stated that "they had both resolved to leave the Pirates the first opportunity and apply themselves to some honest livelihood."

Calico Jack Rackam and eight of his pirates were found guilty and sentenced to be hanged. By "special Favour," Rackam was allowed to see Anne Bonny before his execution. The visit brought him little consolation. Bonny's parting words stunned Calico Jack. She told him that she was "sorry to see him there, but if he had fought like a Man, he need not have been hang'd like a Dog."

Calico Jack, his leg irons clanking on the stone floor, stumbled outside. The waiting guards led him to the scaffold and the hangman's rope. On Friday, November 18, 1720, Captain John Rackam was hanged at Gallows Point at Port Royal. Afterward, his body was put into an iron cage and hung from a gibbet on Deadman's Cay "for a publick Example and to terrify others from such-like evil Practices." Today the small island is called Rackam's Cay.

A week later, Anne Bonny, not yet twenty years old, and Mary Read were tried on the same charges. Additional witnesses testified in the women's trial. Dorothy

By the early eighteenth century, governments were beginning to crack down on piracy across the seas. Calico Jack was hung at Gallows Point in Port Royal, Jamaica, in 1720. (National Maritime Museum, Greenwich, England)

Thomas, who was in a canoe when the pirates attacked her, gave the following description: "The two women prisoners . . . wore men's jackets, and long trousers, and handkerchiefs tied about their heads; and that each of them had a machet and pistol in their hands, and cursed and swore at the men, to murder [Thomas] . . . and the reason of her knowing and believing them to be women then was by the largeness of their breasts."

Thomas Dillon testified that "Anne Bonny, one of the prisoners at the bar, had a gun in her hand, and they were both very profligate, cursing and swearing much, and very ready and willing to do anything on board."

Found guilty of the charges, Anne Bonny and Mary

Read received death sentences. After informing the court that they were both pregnant, the court ordered that "the said sentence should be respited" and an inspection made. The examination proved they were pregnant, and both were reprieved.

Read, spared from execution, contracted fever and died in prison before the birth of her baby. The Parish Register for the district of St. Catherine in Jamaica recorded her burial on April 28, 1721. According to the records, Bonny escaped the hangman's noose. What happened to Anne Bonny or her child remains a mystery.

The Golden Age of Piracy ended a few years after the hanging of Calico Jack Rackam and his crew around 1725. But piracy would never be fully eradicated from the seas.

TIMELINE

1660   Daniel Defoe is born.
1701   The War of the Spanish Succession begins.
1714   George I inherits the throne; the War of the Spanish Succession ends.
1719   *Robinson Crusoe* is published.
1720   Mary Read and Anne Bonny are arrested and tried.
1721   Mary Read dies.
1724   Daniel Defoe, writing as Captain Charles Johnson, publishes *The General History of the Robberies and Murders of the Most Notorious Pyrates.*

RACHEL WALL

Boston Pirate

The story of Rachel Wall, an American woman who was convicted and hanged on Boston Common in 1789, is an example of the small-scale piracy that erupted in the years following the Revolutionary War.

Rachel Wall was born in Carlisle, Pennsylvania, in 1760—the year that brought an end to the French and Indian War. England's victory added Canada to her already vast empire, and England's border now extended all the way to the Mississippi River.

The British Empire's most prized possession remained the thirteen colonies, but problems began to develop there after the French and Indian War. George III became king at the age of twenty-two, and friction developed as the mother country sought ways to impose taxes on the colonies to help pay for England's large war debt.

Although settlers had cleared land for nearly two centuries, America remained a wilderness broken by patches of settlement. A few large cities clustered around the most promising harbors. Towns were small and located great distances apart. Nine out of ten Americans lived off the land.

Rachel Wall's father was a farmer. Growing up on a farm meant hard work for the entire family. Rachel, her three brothers, and two sisters put in long days laboring in the fields. Then there were the daily chores: milking the cows, feeding the farm animals, and gathering eggs.

Rachel described her parents as "honest and reputable." She credited them with giving her a good education and instructing her in the fundamental principles of Christianity: "They . . . taught me the fear of God, and if I had followed the good advice and pious counsel they often gave me, I should never have come to this untimely fate."

Her devout father offered family prayers in his house every morning and evening. On Sunday night, he gathered his family and read from the Bible, pausing to quiz the children on the passages.

The signing of the Declaration of Independence took place when Rachel was sixteen. The Revolutionary War brought additional hardships to the rugged farm life and the dull, dusty village of Carlisle.

The waterfront in Boston, Massachusetts, an important eighteenth-century port, as it looked during the short life of Rachel Wall. (National Maritime Museum, Greenwich, England)

At a young age, Rachel left home without her parents' consent. She returned again and "was received by them, but could not be contented; therefore I tarried with them but two years before I left them again, and I have never seen them since."

The second time, she ran away to Philadelphia with George Wall, a sailor, whom she had married. Wall also had a restless and discontented nature. Leaving Philadelphia, they traveled to New York. Three months later, the Walls headed to Boston.

Soon George went to sea on a fishing schooner, leaving Rachel behind. With George away, Rachel worked as a servant in a fine house in Boston and "lived very contented."

Two months later, George returned. Rachel reported that "as soon as he came back, he enticed me to leave my service and take to bad company, from which I may date my ruin." Besides her husband, the bad company included George's five shipmates and their rowdy female companions. The sailors spent their earnings in less than a week. One night, while George and his friends were out late carousing, the fishing schooner sailed without them.

With no prospects for making money, George suggested to his companions that they become pirates and get rich. During the Revolutionary War, all the men had served aboard privateers, capturing British ships, plundering them, and dividing the spoils with the government as part of the war effort.

George Wall and his cronies knew that piracy in peacetime was a hanging offense. Still, they were unable to resist the temptation of a life of luxury. The sailors agreed to George's plan. Even Rachel accepted the invitation.

George Wall had his pirate crew but no ship. An acquaintance owned a fast fishing schooner but no longer fished because he was an invalid. George persuaded the man to let him borrow the idle schooner, promising him a share of the catch. The pirate crew fished during good weather, selling their catch at Plymouth Harbor. But the first time a storm came up, George put his scheme into action.

George scudded into a small, secluded harbor at the

Isles of Shoals and moored the schooner there to ride out the gale. As the winds subsided, the captain ordered his crew to hoist sail and put out to sea.

When they reached the busy shipping lanes, George Wall shouted to his crew to seize the sails, pull them loose, and twist them for a storm-battered look. Then, he hoisted the distress signal. Rachel, in a tattered dress, was the bait. She stood on the deck, pretending to be a pathetic survivor on the weather-beaten hulk.

The wait was not long. Rachel waved her arms for help as a fishing schooner from Plymouth drew alongside. Only four men were aboard her. The captain, seeing Rachel's condition and the sails torn and hanging slack, offered passage into port for Captain Wall, his wife, and his five-man crew. The scheme had worked.

Once on board the schooner, George gave the signal. He and his men drew their knives and slit the throats of the fishermen. Working on the decks, slippery with blood, the murderers tied weights to the bodies and threw them overboard.

From this escapade, the pirates gained $360 in cash, some expensive fishing gear, and several hundreds of pounds of fish ready for market. They transferred the booty from the Plymouth schooner to the borrowed schooner. Then the crew scuttled the Plymouth boat. Nothing remained as the waves washed over the last of the sinking ship.

The pirates returned to the Isles of Shoals. A few days later, they went into Plymouth to sell the stolen fishing

Because of its convenient port and proximity to busy trading routes, the town of Plymouth, Massachusetts, where the Mayflower *had landed in 1620, was a popular place for pirates to sell and spend their spoils.* (Library of Congress)

gear. They explained that it had washed up on the shore after the big storm.

Five weeks later, a hurricane struck the New England coast. Captain Wall and his crew set out to sea in the storm's wake. They sighted a trading vessel. Rachel donned her tattered clothes again and stood at the rail, waving frantically for help.

This time, the rescue ship was a sloop from Penobscot with a crew of seven. Instead of accepting their kind offer to come aboard, Wall shouted to the captain that he wanted to stay with his ship to try to make repairs. He invited the captain and a mate to come aboard to help stop a leak. The two men descended into the hold. Wall and one of his crew thrust a knife into each man's back.

This painting, by Auguste-François Biard, shows pirates dressed as women and harmless civilians in order to trick a passing ship into allowing them to come alongside and attack. Pirates commonly used cunning and disguise, as well as signals of distress, as ploys to lure their prey. (National Maritime Museum, Greenwich, England)

Going above deck, George called to the other vessel that their captain needed some wedges. Two sailors brought the wedges over and took them below, where they were killed. The three remaining seamen met similar deaths. Seven murders produced a profit of $550 from the captain's chest and $870 from the sale of merchandise.

The Walls continued to prey on vessels into the next year. The raids provided a steady income—though by no means the wealth they anticipated. George seemed to have an uncanny sense of the moment when a storm had subsided—the right moment to set sail.

One summer day, anchored at their usual spot off the Isles of Shoals, they waited for a hurricane to pass. The sun came out briefly. Captain Wall ordered his men to set sail.

They reached open sea just as the howling wind and rain returned in all their fury. No pretending this time— this distress was real. What he had assumed to be the end of the storm was the calm at the eye of the hurricane. For the first time, he had misjudged the weather. Rain pelted the crew as they tried to adjust the sails. Mountainous waves cascaded over the bow, causing the fishing schooner to buck and toss like a giant seesaw. Then a sound like the boom of a cannon pierced the air.

Terrified, Rachel watched as the mainmast snapped in two. George clung to the rigging with one hand, but the sheer force of the surging waves swept the crewman beside him overboard. As the storm intensified, the waves increased in size. One mighty billow enveloped George, wresting his hand loose and pushing him over the rail into the yawning dark chasm.

The next day, a brig from New York rescued the

survivors. For the first time, Rachel Wall's distress was sincere.

That marked the end of piracy for Rachel Wall.

The ship dropped her off at Boston, where she returned to her old job as a servant in Beacon Hill. But she could not stop lying and stealing. For her, the risk of being apprehended increased the excitement. Knowing the places where money and valuables were hidden on board ships had become second nature to Rachel during her days of piracy.

She formed the habit of slipping down to the waterfront late at night and boarding ships. A good place to search for valuables was the captain's head—the latrine reserved for the exclusive use of the master of the ship. In the spring of 1787, she went aboard a ship lying at the Long Wharf in Boston. She recollected that

> on my entering the cabin, the door of which not being fastened, and finding the Captain and Mate asleep in their beds, I hunted about for plunder, and discovered under the Captain's head, a black silk handkerchief containing upwards of thirty pounds in gold crowns and small change, on which I immediately seized the booty and decamped therewith as quick as possible, which money I spent freely . . . full proving the old adage, "Light come, light go."

On another occasion, Rachel broke into a sloop anchored at Doane's Wharf. She found the captain and every hand on board asleep: "I looked round to see what

I could help myself to, when I spied a silver watch hanging over the Captain's head, which I pocketed. I also took a pair of silver buckles out of the Captain's shoes: I likewise made free with a parcel of small change for pocket money, to make myself merry among my evil companions and made my escape without being discovered."

Rachel even confessed to a robbery that another poor wretch was supposed to have committed: "I . . . declare Miss Dorothy Horn, a crippled person in Boston Alms House, to be entirely innocent of the theft at Mr. Vaughn's in Essex-Street, tho' she suffered a long imprisonment, was set on the gallows one hour and whipped five stripes therefor."

Along with housing a merchants' exchange and the Massachusetts Assembly, Boston's Old State House (front left) *was home to the Massachusetts Supreme Judicial Court and the Courts of Suffolk County. It is likely that Rachel Wall was tried for her crimes within this historic building.* (Library of Congress)

A woodcut depicting the execution of Rachel Wall, along with several others.
(Library of Congress)

If one believes this light-fingered woman's dying confession, she was never caught at any of the crimes she committed, and she did not commit the offense for which she was finally caught and charged.

According to her story, on her way home one evening after work, "without design to injure any person," Rachel heard a noise in the street. Details of the incident are sketchy. With Rachel's penchant for pilfering, it is easy to imagine that she could not control the overpowering urge to snatch a fancy bonnet off the head of an expensively dressed young girl walking toward her. Striking the young woman to the ground, she allegedly jammed the girl's bonnet on her own head and fled, but she was unable to outrun a pursuing officer.

Rachel Wall was tried on September 10, 1789. The charge delivered to the jury was that "she feloniously did assault and take from the person of Margaret Bender, one bonnet of the value of seven shillings."

Although she admitted on the witness stand to being a pirate and a thief, she insisted that in her pirate days she never murdered anyone. She protested her innocence of the robbery charge to the last. The verdict handed down was that she be returned to jail to await execution. There was no appeal from a defense counsel, no public protest, nor any request for a stay of execution.

On the day of the hanging, October 7, 1789, the maple trees encircling Boston Common were a riot of color. A crowd gathered early. According to the spectators, Rachel's face appeared to be carved in stone. She chose not to say any last words. Maybe she was thinking of the last words of confession she had made just a few hours earlier: "And now into the hands of Almighty God I commit my soul, relying on his mercy, through the merits and meditations of my Redeemer, and die an unworthy member of the Presbyterian Church in the 29th year of my age."

Pirate Rachel Wall was the last woman hanged at Boston Common.

TIMELINE

1760   Rachel Wall is born in Carlisle, Pennsylvania; French and Indian War ends; George III ascends to the British throne.

1775   Shots exchanged at the battles of Lexington and Concord.

1776   Declaration of Independence signed.

1781   British general Charles Cornwallis surrenders at Yorktown and the American Revolution ends.

1789   George Washington is elected president; Rachel Wall is tried, convicted, and hanged.

FANNY CAMPBELL

Revolutionary Pirate

S'uppose someone said to you, "I possess knowledge concerning your ancestors which you might not wish to discover. If you so desire, I will share this knowledge. If not, the information dies with me." How would you respond?

In 1917, Dr. Charles Edward Lovell posed this question to a relative, John Austin Belden of Wareham, Massachusetts. Unable to contain his curiosity, Belden said, "Come on, Charles, let's have it."

Dr. Lovell disclosed that one of Belden's ancestors had turned pirate more that one hundred years before and was never apprehended. He explained that the entire story, written in a pamphlet, was in his possession, and if John Belden would like to know its contents, he would will it to him.

Following Dr. Lovell's death in October 1930, John Belden received the document. He hastened upstairs. There he opened the envelope that contained not only the astounding history of Fanny Campbell, his great-great-grandmother, but a drawing of her in color. Beldon was rapt as the story of his ancestor unfolded before his eyes.

The Campbell family lived next to the Lovells at the base of High Rock in Lynn, Massachusetts, a small town north of Boston. As Fanny matured, she fell in love with William Lovell, who was a year older. William loved Fanny, though she wasn't like most girls. Fanny rode horses and was a sharpshooter who killed panthers in Lynn Woods. She knew all about sailing and could handle a sailboat as well as a man.

Fanny Campbell was eighteen and William Lovell nineteen when what later became known as the Boston Tea Party took place. On Monday, December 20, 1773, the *Boston Gazette* reported: "A number of brave & resolute men . . . emptied every chest of tea on board . . . amounting to 342 chests into the sea!" This led King George III to impose further restrictions on the colony of Massachusetts.

About this time, William Lovell, who enjoyed sailing and fishing, decided to become a deep-sea sailor. For six months, he sailed aboard a New England merchant ship, returning tanned and more mature. The changes in her young friend, and Lovell's exciting tales of visits to foreign lands, fascinated Campbell. She confided to

Citizens of Boston, some disguised as Native Americans, boarded ships in Boston Harbor and threw chests of tea overboard on December 18, 1773. The Boston Tea Party, incited by the colonists' anger at Britain's policy of "taxation without represen-tation," is considered one of the benchmark events in the American Revolution. (Library of Congress)

Lovell that she, too, yearned to make an ocean voyage.

On the eve of his second sailing, the two young lovers climbed to the top of High Rock. They talked of the future. Lovell explained that, although he had a chance to sail aboard the *Royal Kent* bound for South America and the Indies, he would leave the sea if she wished. Campbell urged him to go ahead and work until he was captain of his own ship.

William Lovell sailed the next day. He was away for two years. During that time, Campbell had another caller. Captain Robert Burnet was an officer in the British Navy assigned to a British warship anchored in Boston Har-bor. At first, Captain Burnet showed only a casual inter-est in Campbell. Later, his attentiveness turned to love.

The schooner, a popular pirate vessel in North America during the time of the American Revolution, uses fore-and-aft sails on two or more masts, with the forward mast being shorter or the same height as the rear masts. (Library of Congress)

But Campbell waited for Lovell. Far at sea, William Lovell thought of the girl back in Lynn and determined to marry her on his return voyage.

When a pirate schooner displaying the skull and crossbones loomed on the horizon, the captain of Lovell's ship ordered all hands to prepare the cannons for defense. BOOM! BOOM! BOOM! The six-pounders caused damage, but the sea ruffians continued to come nearer and nearer. The bearded, sunburned pirates, armed with cutlasses and pistols, threw grapnels across to the *Royal Kent* and boarded her. In a short time, the sea bandits overwhelmed the American sailors.

In the skirmish, the captain of the *Royal Kent* killed the pirate leader. But moments later, one of the pirates ran a sword through the American captain. The pirates killed more than twice the number they lost. The remaining pirates forced the American survivors to join their ranks. The pirates then scuttled the *Royal Kent.*

Lovell, seriously wounded in the battle, watched as the *Royal Kent* sank to the bottom of the ocean. After his recovery, he assumed an active role in sailing the pirate craft.

The pirates went ashore at Tortuga Island in the Caribbean. Each man buried his share of the loot taken from the *Royal Kent* in a secret hiding place away from his fellow pirates.

Soon after, the pirates went to sea again. They headed toward Cuba. Before reaching that island, the wind died. Their craft lay becalmed. Lovell and two companions, Jack Herbert and Henry Breed, were assigned the night watch.

The three New Englanders decided to make a getaway. They headed the schooner into the light wind that had sprung up and tied the wheel so the ship would stay on course. Slipping a small boat over the side, they lowered a few provisions and scrambled down a rope ladder into the dinghy.

The sailors rowed desperately until they were out of range of the pirates. When the breeze freshened, they hoisted sail for Havana. Eventually, the dirty and ragged sailors, elated by their escape from the pirates, reached the Cuban capital.

Fanny Campbell, disguised as a man, sailed into Havana, Cuba, to rescue her future husband. (Courtesy of the Granger Collection.)

Their joy was short-lived. Cuban officials arrested the three Americans on suspicion of being pirates and threw them into jail since they had no proof of being forced aboard the pirate ship. They waited week after week for their trial. Six months passed before they appeared in court where, with no evidence against them, the judge ordered them returned to their cells.

Back in Massachusetts, Fanny Campbell longed for word from Lovell. Months went by. Captain Burnet continued his visits. Fanny remained true to William.

In Havana, after two years in prison, Lovell's friend Jack Herbert escaped and made his way to an American ship at the pier. After telling his story, he received permission to hide aboard the vessel and sail back to Boston.

Shortly after landing, Jack Herbert delivered a dirty, crumpled letter to Campbell from Lovell. Clutching the unexpected missive, Campbell questioned Herbert about the Cuban prison. He described it as heavily guarded.

Before Herbert left, Campbell obtained his address. She told him to be ready at a moment's notice for a strange adventure that might take place at any time, day or night. Although mystified by her secretive manner, Jack Herbert agreed.

The following evening, Captain Burnet called on Campbell and learned that Lovell was still alive. Fanny convinced Burnet that Lovell was the one for her. His hopes dashed, the disappointed captain left.

One week later, a man dressed as a sailor knocked on

Jack Herbert's door and reminded him of his promise to Fanny Campbell. Following the man's instructions, Herbert, posing as a common sailor, went aboard the heavily armed *Constance,* anchored in Boston Harbor. She was set to sail for England by way of Cuba.

The captain of the *Constance* was a tyrant named Brownless. The first mate, Banning, was a dimwit. The second officer was an unusual character named Channing, who had joined the crew the day before. The men admired him for his ease onboard ship. Channing knew something the crew did not. Captain Brownless planned to press the entire crew into the British navy once they reached England. Channing decided to use the captain's scheme to his advantage.

When the *Constance* was about a day's sail from Cuba, Channing went to the captain's cabin. Seizing a brace of pistols from the captain's table and a cutlass from the bulkhead, Channing confronted the captain.

"Captain Brownless, you are my prisoner!"

The captain muttered, "Mutiny!" With his weapons gone, however, he had little choice. Channing tied up the captain, locked him in his quarters, and ordered Jack Herbert to call the crew aft.

With the crew assembled on deck, Channing explained the captain's devious plot to press every sailor into the British navy. The men cheered to signify their acceptance of Channing as the new captain.

All was not well, however. The ship's British cook was making plans to kill Channing. Meanwhile, Brownless managed to escape his cabin, intent on the same bloody errand. The two men met in the darkness outside the entrance to Channing's quarters and, mistaking each other for Channing, engaged in deadly combat. The following morning, a crewmember stumbled upon their bodies. The remains of the two men were dropped over the side of the ship.

The *Constance,* now a pirate craft with Channing as captain, overpowered a British bark, the *George.* Jack Herbert was given command of the new ship.

A few days later, as the ships sailed side by side, mutiny broke out aboard the *George.* Captain Channing watched from the other craft as Herbert was roped and thrown on the deck. Crossing over at once in a small boat, Channing boarded the vessel with drawn pistols, killed one of the mutineers, and put an end to the mutiny.

Late one night, the two ships sailed into Havana Bay. Channing ordered Jack Herbert to pick eight loyal crew members and tell them about the fort where Lovell and Breed were prisoners.

Herbert and the eight sailors rowed to the fort. Leaving one man to guard the rowboat, the others crawled along the sandy beach. They sighted a mute form ahead. A Spanish sentry! Sneaking to the rear of the guard, a sailor silenced forever the unfortunate Spaniard. Three more sentries met the same fate. The sailors locked the four bodies in the guardhouse.

Using keys taken from the guards, Herbert sneaked into the jail and awakened Lovell and Breed. The men sprinted out, and an hour later, all eleven Americans were in the small boat, rowing desperately for the brig. Just as the two vessels set sail, they heard the unmistakable roll of the fort drums, signaling the discovery of the escape. But it was too late. The American ships sailed away from shore and out of danger.

Channing appointed William Lovell first mate of the *Constance*. Several days later, the captain called Lovell to his cabin and revealed to the astonished sailor that Captain Channing was in reality Fanny Campbell. Fanny's disguise—skin dyed brown, hair cropped short, and wearing a marine officer's uniform—had served her well. Even Lovell failed to recognize her. Campbell cautioned him against letting the crew know her secret.

The *Constance* and the *George* continued their voyage uneventfully until they met and seized a British merchant ship. They learned from the crew that the Revolutionary War was in full swing. To escape the stigma of piracy, Fanny persuaded the sailors to give up their pirating ways and turn privateer. Now, instead of robbing any ship that came along for their own profit, the crews of the two crafts would work for the American government, capturing only enemy ships and turning a share of the booty over to the Continental Congress.

Soon, the *Constance* and the *George* captured a British armed sloop. It was quite a shock to Campbell when the captain of the sloop turned out to be her former suitor, Captain Burnet. He was shackled below deck along with the other prisoners. Although Captain Burnet recognized Campbell, he did not reveal her identity.

When Campbell learned from the prisoners that the British now occupied Boston, she set a course for Marblehead, Massachusetts. There, the crews of the *Constance* and the *George* became legal privateers of the new nation. They received "letters of marque" or commissions, carrying on the centuries old tradition of allowing citizens to attack and plunder enemy ships during wartime.

During the Revolution, Congress issued 1,700 letters

A British warship gives chase to a three-masted pirate lugger. The lugger can be seen flying the Jolly Roger on the aft-most mast, called the mizzenmast. (Library of Congress)

of marque and reprisal. The Atlantic coast, with its hundreds of bays and inlets and scores of rivers emptying into the ocean, was ideal for privateering.

Sailors signed aboard a privateer out of a mixture of anger, need, and greed. They made more than a thousand dollars in just one British prize, at a time when families lived comfortably on nine dollars a month.

For all of its promise of wealth, privateering was risky. British warships captured hordes of American privateers. Since they were not in the armed forces, they were not considered prisoners of war. In British eyes, they were pirates who could not be hanged for fear of reprisal. The British solved the problem by keeping them in conditions in which many would die anyhow. They converted large old warships into floating dungeons. The hulks, stripped of sails and fittings and with boarded up portholes, kept the prisoners completely sealed in except for small slits cut in the ships' sides for air. When they had food, it was spoiled and crawling with insects. According to a prisoner who survived, the water was "an astonishing greenish-yellow that had a foul, sour smell."

Over 13,000 Americans—more than the total killed in George Washington's army—died of disease and starvation aboard the filthy, rat-infested floating prisons. Privateers who avoided the hulks captured and brought in over 3,000 British ships, most of them merchant vessels.

Before heading back to sea as a privateer, Lovell married Campbell. As far as we know, Fanny Campbell never went to sea again.

Lovell served his country as a privateer until the war ended. Later, he made several long trips to China and then retired from the sea.

William and Fanny Lovell had a large family. Apparently, at the time their sons and daughters were growing up, it was common knowledge that Fanny turned pirate to rescue her loved one. But over time, her story was nearly lost to history—that is, until Charles Lovell's startling revelation.

There is a final postscript to the tale of Fanny Campbell. After John Belden read his ancestor's story, he discovered in a collection of whaling logs and scrimshaws a whale's tooth with a picture of a female pirate etched upon it. Belden's portrait of his great-great-grandmother matched the picture on the whale's tooth exactly.

TIMELINE

1760 George III ascends to the British throne.
1773 The Boston Tea Party occurs.
1775 Shots exchanged at the battles of Lexington and Concord.
1776 Declaration of Independence signed.
1781 British general Charles Cornwallis surrenders at Yorktown and the American Revolution ends.
1789 George Washington is elected president.
1930 John Belden inherits a pamphlet revealing his ancestor's deeds.

CHENG I SAO

Chinese Pirate and Warlord

After piracy had virtually ceased elsewhere in the world, it still flourished in the South China Sea. Piracy was by no means new to the region. Its beginnings date back to the fourth century BCE. But famine, overpopulation, increased maritime trade, and weak government accounted for the rise in piracy in the early 1800s.

Bloodthirsty sailors roamed the rivers and coastal waters in junks—flat-bottomed boats designed for speed and ease of navigation in shallow waters. In 1809, a Chinese admiral said, "The pirates are too powerful, we cannot master them by our arms."

The most powerful pirate of all was a woman, Cheng I Sao. At one time, she commanded a fleet of 2,000 junks and 70,000 men and women. Most of the information

A typical early-nineteenth-century junk of the South China Sea. (Library of Congress)

about her life comes from a Chinese chronicle based on firsthand information of the pirates and their activities that was published during Cheng I Sao's lifetime. Also, a number of captives recorded for posterity their experiences aboard the pirate ships.

During the first decade of the nineteenth century, the waters around Canton, Macao, and Hong Kong were thick with pirate junks. Piracy was a struggle to survive —with a revolutionary tinge. Hordes of impoverished fishermen, locked into recurring cycles of debt, and dockworkers unable to make a living joined forces with the pirates, plundering ships and waging war on corrupt Mandarin rule.

Most of the rank and file of the pirates must have seen piracy as a means to trade their drab existence on shore for a life of adventure. Many were driven by the desire to escape the tyranny of officials and taxes. However, the majority who turned to piracy went in search of profit.

Many women participated in their husband's piracy. Most of the propelling and sculling of the lighter vessels was regarded as women's work. But they also took part in combat.

In 1801, the pirate leader Cheng I took a wife. His family had been involved in piracy since the late seventeenth century. Cheng I, a hunchback and the son of a peasant, was forced to go to sea because his father couldn't afford to feed him. He turned pirate and engaged in sporadic attacks on oceangoing traders. Cheng I's sea robbers also made raids inland, including slaves in their booty.

When the time came that Cheng I was ready to take a wife, twenty captured females, bound hand and foot, were brought before him. One of the women was Hsi Kai, a graceful peasant girl, with skin "of the tint of rich cream but at the cheek became a deep rose. Her eyes were black and would shine like jet, and the same black sheen was in her hair." It is said that "before the beauty of her face, the eyes of men grew confused."

Dazzled by this stunning creature, Cheng I had her untied. Her feet were not deformed by binding as prescribed by Chinese custom. The moment she was set free, Hsi Kai lunged at the fat old pirate chief, almost scratching his eyes out before being pulled away. Despite her aggressive temperament, Cheng I offered her jewels, cosmetics, brightly colored silks, and slaves if she would consent to be his wife.

In what was a bold move for a Chinese woman, she demanded—and got—a half-share of his wealth, in addition to joint command of his pirate fleet. Cheng I and his wife emerged as leaders of a successful pirate confederation composed of six principal fleets.

Hsi Kai became Cheng I Sao—her name means "wife of Cheng I." She assisted her husband in the creation of the confederation. Colored banners of red, yellow, blue, green, black, and white distinguished the Chengs' fleets.

As a squadron commander, Cheng I Sao demonstrated skill, cunning, and leadership. Her strategy was to take the enemy by surprise and overpower them in hand-to-hand combat. She usually concealed most of her vessels behind a promontory—a long strip of land jutting into the sea—and sent out two or three as decoys. After the initial contact with a likely target, the remaining ships would emerge to surround the boat.

Their most lethal weapons were bamboo pikes with sharp, saber-like blades of varying lengths. Large boats filled with straw were set ablaze. The winds tormented the flames to fury as these floating fireballs made their way into the fleets of their adversaries. The pirates hurled smaller firebrands out of long hollow bamboo stalks, aimed at enemy sails.

At times, the pirates went into battle with faces aflame

This lively illustration of Cheng I Sao in action was drawn during her life.
(National Maritime Museum, Greenwich, England)

and eyes aglow as a result of drinking a mixture of wine and gunpowder. To bolster their courage, they sometimes ate the hearts of vanquished foes. In combat, they repeatedly sprinkled themselves with garlic water as a charm to ward off bullets.

The pirates preferred to operate in the less treacherous coastal waters. They also plundered villages, markets, and rice fields on shore, assisted by local bandits. By late 1805, pirate-bandit raids occurred regularly.

On December 7, 1806, John Turner, chief mate of the

The capture of John Turner, chief mate of the Tay, *by Cheng I's pirates in 1806.*
(National Maritime Museum, Greenwich, England)

Tay, was captured by Cheng I. He was held for ransom for five months and wrote an account of his captivity. He estimated the Chengs' fleet as between five and six hundred vessels divided into six squadrons. Each operated individually in its own allotted area off the China coast. In major expeditions, the squadrons banded together. The bigger junks carried twelve guns as well as rowboats armed with swivel guns.

Turner's food consisted of skimpy portions of coarse red rice and occasionally some salt fish. He described the conditions on board ship as "wretched": "At night the space allowed me to sleep in was never more than about eighteen inches wide, and four feet long; and if at any time I happened to extend my contracted limbs beyond their limits, I was sure to be reminded of my mistake by a blow or kick."

Before his release in 1807, John Turner suffered cruel treatment and witnessed some gruesome scenes. He described the fate of a Chinese naval officer: "I saw one man . . . nailed to the deck through his feet with large nails, then beaten with four rattans twisted together, till he vomited blood; and after remaining some time in this state, he was taken ashore and cut to pieces."

The same year Turner was freed, Cheng I Sao's husband was lost at sea in a storm. When the Chinese pirates gathered to elect a new leader, Cheng I Sao arrived dressed in the chief's uniform: "embroidered dragons writhed over" the robe of purple, blue, red, and gold. In her sash, she wore "some of her dead husband's swords." On her head was "his familiar war helmet."

"Look at me, captains," she said to the assembled group. "Your departed chief sat in council with me. Your most powerful fleet, the White, under my command, took more prizes than any other. Do you think I will bow to any other chief?"

And so Cheng I Sao, instead of retiring to chaste widowhood, became head of the pirate hierarchy.

In her first act as chief, she appointed twenty-one-year-old Chang Pao, her "adopted" son, commander of the Red Flag fleet. Chang Pao (also referred to as Paou), a fisherman's son, had joined the pirates at age fifteen after being captured by Cheng I, who "liked him so much, that he could not depart from him" and eventually made him commander of a ship. In time, Chang Pao became the lover and, later, the husband of Cheng I Sao.

Cheng I Sao ruled her fleet with an iron fist. She required her men to adhere to a code of conduct that regulated all aspects of their lives. This code was harsh and kept the men united and well disciplined. Any seaman who went ashore without permission would have his ears slit; a repetition of the same unlawful act meant death. Mistreatment of a woman prisoner resulted in execution. Stealing from village suppliers and pilfering from the common treasury were also capital offenses.

All loot was entered on the warehouse register. Cheng I Sao operated on such a large scale that, unlike the usual practice of pirates, she required written records. Any pirate wishing to draw from the common fund made a written application to the secretary of the storehouse, who was called the Ink and Writing Master.

Like the other boat dwellers of the South China Sea, the pirates prayed to their gods before each foray. If reports from the gods were unfavorable, they would not undertake a mission. The flamboyant Chang Pao, who usually dressed in a purple silk robe and a black turban, had a magnificent temple constructed aboard his largest ship.

Under the pirate confederation, captives were a significant source of manpower. One government official

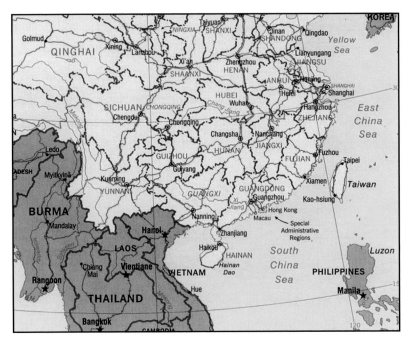

Cheng I Sao and her organization pirated in the South China Sea off the coast of Hong Kong.

estimated that captives made up more than half of the entire force, and most of them served the pirates without any hope of release.

Chinese pirates captured Richard Glasspoole, an officer on the East India Company ship *Marquis of Ely,* and seven British seafarers on September 21, 1809. Until his release on December 7, Glasspoole kept a diary of life on board a pirate junk.

Glasspoole wrote that the pirates "have no settled residence on shore, but live constantly in their vessels." Every man was allowed "a small berth about four feet square" to stow his wife and family. "From the number of souls crowded in so small a space," he reported, "it must naturally be supposed they are horribly dirty, which is evidently the case, and their vessels swarm with all kinds of vermin."

According to Glasspoole, certain species of rats, encouraged to breed, were eaten as "great delicacies." He noted there were "very few creatures" they would not eat: "During our captivity we lived three weeks on caterpillars boiled with rice!" Glasspoole's account describes the pirates as being "much addicted to gambling." Their leisure hours were spent "at cards and smoking opium." Glasspoole and his men witnessed entire villages being destroyed and men, women, and children being massacred. The Englishmen were forced to participate in the carnage.

A Chinese historian describes a battle between the pirates and the villagers of Kan-shih. As the pirates made their way into the village, one hundred women hid in the surrounding paddy fields. When a baby's wail gave them away, the pirates captured the women and children. One of the women, Mei Ying, "was very beautiful, and a pirate being about to seize her by the head, she abused him exceedingly." In the skirmish, "the pirate dragged her down and broke two of her teeth, which filled her mouth and jaws with blood." As the pirate approached her again, "she laid hold of his garments with her bleeding mouth and threw both him and herself into the river where they were drowned."

Cheng I Sao's financial operation included a protection racket whereby she sold safe passage protection on land as well as sea. During September 1809, Richard Glasspoole accompanied the pirates on one of their fee-collecting missions. Five hundred junks sailed up the Pearl River. Glasspoole's boat anchored close to a vil-

A skirmish between pirate junks and British Royal Navy steamships on the South China Sea. (National Maritime Museum, Greenwich, England)

lage. The crews burned the customs house and readied their rowboats for attack.

A messenger went into the village and demanded a payment of $10,000 annually. When payment was refused, the pirates threatened to destroy the town and murder all the inhabitants. The two sides finally agreed on a fee of $6,000, "which they were to collect by the time of our return down the river," says Glasspoole.

On October 1, 1909, Glasspoole witnessed the capture of 250 women and children. It was a "melancholy sight to see women in tears, clasping their infants in their arms and imploring mercy for them from those brutal robbers. . . . They were unable to escape with the men owing to that abominable practice of cramping their feet. . . . In fact, they might all be said to totter, rather than walk." He notes that "twenty of the female captives were brought on board the ship on which I was." They were hauled on board by the hair and treated in a most savage manner. Several of the women "leaped overboard and drowned themselves" rather than submit to the horrific abuse.

One of Glasspoole's sailors was rounding a corner during a skirmish when he met a pirate with a "drawn sword in his hand" and " two Chinamen's heads" tied by their pigtails slung around his neck. He was chasing a third victim. On this occasion, Chang Pao had offered ten dollars for every head produced.

Finally, Richard Glasspoole and his men were ransomed for a handsome sum and delivered from "a miserable captivity, which we had endured for eleven weeks and three days."

At the time of Glasspoole's liberation, the confederation was at the height of its power. Yet the association survived only a few months longer. Dissension broke out among the pirates. Then, in a complete turnabout, the Chinese emperor, unable to conquer the pirates, offered amnesty. Like that offered by European rulers, the settlement included a pardon, money, and land to any pirate who would surrender.

Cheng I Sao understood the advantages of the offer. On April 18, 1810, leading a delegation of seventeen women and children, she went unarmed to the governor-general in Canton to negotiate. Two days later the surrender took place.

Throughout her career as a pirate, Cheng I Sao had expanded the pirate empire her husband built. The confederation prospered as she won the support of her followers, issued orders, planned military campaigns, and exercised her business acumen.

Less than a decade after the dismantling of the confederation, Chang Pao rose to the post of colonel in the military. Cheng I Sao made this high position possible. Chang Pao died at the age of thirty-six, ending the spectacular rise of this illiterate fisherman's son.

Cheng I Sao, widowed a second time, spent her last days in Canton, "leading a peaceful life so far as consistent with the keeping of an infamous gambling house." She died in 1844 at the age of sixty-nine.

TIMELINE

1775   Hsi Kai (later Cheng I Sao) born.
1776   American Declaration of Independence is signed.
1801   Hsi Kai and Cheng I are married.
1806   John Turner is captured and begins writing a record of his time as a prisoner.
1807   Turner is released; Cheng I Sao is elected commander in chief after her husband's death.
1809   Richard Glasspoole is captured and begins his own diary.
1844   Cheng I Sao dies.

LAI CHOI SAN

Twentieth-Century Pirate

While on land, Lai Choi San dressed in expensive garments of white silk and wore costly jade earrings. Her jet-black hair was "twisted in a knot" and fastened with gleaming jade pins at the nape of her neck. Her jade jewelry matched her green silk slippers. On board ship, she donned pirating clothes—loose pants and a jacket-like top—and preferred to remain barefoot. This modern-day pirate lived and worked in the Macao and Hong Kong areas of southeast China in the 1920s.

Lai Choi San operated in a very different world from the one Cheng I Sao knew one hundred years before. The coming of steam ships meant that Chinese pirates, with their sail-powered vessels, could no longer give chase to faster Western ships. They had to develop new tech-

The waterfront of Hong Kong in the 1920s, during the time when Lai Choi San used the harbor as one of her home ports. (Library of Congress)

niques, such as taking over ships from within. One observer noted, "The Chinese pirates have adapted themselves to modern conditions. They work from a safe base ashore, they have an elaborate intelligence system, and they combine subtlety with force of arms."

Posing as passengers, ten to sixty of Lai Choi San's pirates would board the target ship at dockside. Some traveled first class, often wearing "European clothes and tortoise-shell-rimmed spectacles." The majority of the pirates sailed in third class. They smuggled guns onto the ship with the help of dockworkers. Before the ship sailed, the pirates placed themselves in strategic locations aboard, ready to hijack the vessel when it was well out to sea. The signal to attack was a fierce "beating of the gongs."

The attacks were well organized. One group of the

robbers would storm the bridge while a second group attacked the engine room and a third group kept the passengers at bay. Once the pirates gained control, they brought the ship to Bias Bay and unloaded its cargo into waiting sampans and junks. The cargo promptly disappeared inland, out of the reach of authorities. Once the ship's cargo was unloaded and its rich passengers had been held for ransom, it was then permitted to return to Hong Kong or continue its voyage.

Aleko E. Lilius was a newspaper reporter sent to China to investigate the increased hijackings of American and European vessels. After long negotiations, Lai Choi San allowed the journalist to put out to sea on her ship in exchange for forty-three dollars per day. Jubilant, Lilius wrote:

> Here was I, an American journalist, getting the chance of a lifetime, to sail with Chinese pirates to the central nest of the most merciless gang of high-seas robbers of the world, in an armoured junk commanded by a female pirate. Small wonder that I could hardly believe in my luck.

An unnamed American who had sailed the Macao waters for fifteen years without ever having seen the famous pirate lady told Lilius:

> Undoubtedly she is the Queen of the Macao pirates. . . . I have almost doubted her existence. . . . She is said to have inherited the business and the ships from her

> father, after the old man had gone to his ancestors.
> . . . The authorities had given him some sort of
> refuge here in Macao, with the secret understanding
> that he should protect the colony's enormous fishing
> fleets and do general police duty on the high seas.
> . . . He owned seven fully-armoured junks when he
> died. Today Lai Choi San owns twelve junks. . . .
> She has barrels of money, and her will is law. . . .
> She is said to be both ruthless and cruel. . . . When
> she climbs aboard any of her ships there is an ill-
> wind blowing for someone.

Once on board, Lilius found it hard to believe that he "was actually tramping the deck of an honest-to-goodness pirate ship!" He described the crew as wearing wide-brimmed hats with red kerchiefs tied around their necks: "These fellows were almost giants—muscular, heavy-chested, half-naked, hard-looking—real bandit types." Slowly, they raised the armoured junk's brown sails against the orange dawn sky.

Gazing at the weaponry on board, Lilius wondered if he would return unharmed. The ship carried twelve ancient-looking cannons and two rather modern ones: "The ammunition, both powder and shot, was kept amidships, the heavier shot being stored in a magazine just abaft the foremast. Rifles and pistols were kept in a separate cabin on the poop, next to the captain's quarters."

Still trying to take in his surroundings, Lilius watched as Lai Choi San—whom he referred to as "Madame"—

One of the only known existing images of the pirate Lai Choi San. (From I Sailed with Chinese Pirates by Aleko Lilius.)

stepped on board. The commander went straight to her cabin on the poop. The cabin was the size of "an ordinary grand piano box." Furnished like a small temple, it contained the portrait of a sea goddess and relics of Lai Choi San's father. In this room, Lai Choi San burned incense and meditated for hours with her two maidservants. The cabin was off limits to the male crew members. Her servants delivered her orders to the men in the fleet—Lai Choi San never spoke directly to the men.

On the first afternoon at sea, the journalist experienced the pirates in action. Lai Choi San gave orders to sail toward a large black junk with three yellow sails gleaming in the sunshine. "As soon as the junk recognized us it turned and fled, but we rapidly overtook it. Our crew had brought out the rifles and had put on cartridge belts, and so had Madame." When the fleeing junk was in hearing distance, one of the pirates fired a rifle shot. Lilius expected bullets to be flying about their deck, but nothing really exciting happened.

After much shouting back and forth between the two junks, the skipper of the other boat came over and went below to the captain's quarters. Sometime later, he emerged and returned to his ship. Lilius noted that the pirate captain looked happy, leaving the reporter to wonder how much money the visit had earned him. He wrote, "Apparently, the business had been settled to the satisfaction of everyone concerned."

During the activity, Lai Choi San had continued to sit with her servants at her observation post, "an empty

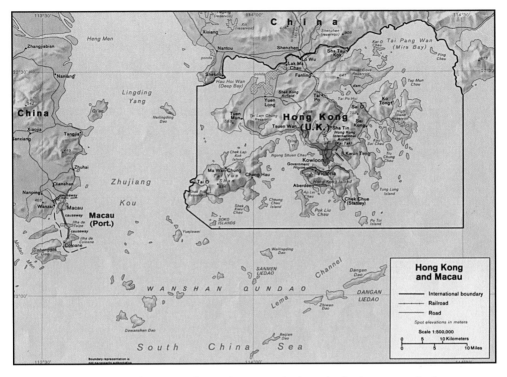

The port cities of Macao and Hong Kong were both run by foreign powers during Lai Choi San's lifetime.

packing case on the top deck of the two-story poop," as if she were completely oblivious to the deliberations taking place. That same afternoon, Lai Choi San's crew chased two more junks, with the same result. After each visit, "the captain's smile became broader and broader."

In conversation over the next few days, Lilius learned that Lai Choi San and her crew practiced a kind of extortion as well, promising fishermen and other merchants protection from other pirates in exchange for payment. But Lai Choi San was not the only pirate in this racket, and some locals found themselves paying protection money to two or three pirates.

Lai Choi San knew some of these other pirate syndicates were conspiring against her. When her captain saw three of their junks riding at anchor in a small bay, he yelled to Lilius to go below. Knowing not to challenge the captain, he obeyed. It was too dark to see, but Lilius could hear clearly the noise from above:

> The whole junk shook with a salvo from our guns. The noise was deafening. Boom! There went another! And a third, a fourth, a fifth and a sixth! A regular bombardment—but there were no reply shots. The enemy never got a chance to fire back. It was indeed a one-sided affair.

An hour after the firing had stopped, the hatch opened and Lilius ventured on deck. Some distance away to the starboard, he saw "the sinking hull of the junk." On deck, he spied two men bound hand and foot. He learned that they were enemy captains being held for ransom. The pirates expected several hundred dollars per head for their return. If Lai Choi San did not receive a ransom upon demand, the prisoner's fingers or ears would be cut off and sent to his relatives. If the ransom remained unpaid, the hostage would be killed. In this instance, the villagers paid the ransom and the reporter "actually saw the captain show Lai Choi San a fat roll of bills."

Lilius wrote that during the course of the journey, Lai Choi San, through an interpreter, told him about her early life:

Her father had four sons, but they were all dead. She had been his only daughter, and being a frail and delicate child had not been expected to live. Her father used to take her with him on his trips along the coast, regarding her more as a servant than as a child of his own. And now she loved the sea.

The old man had started his life, penniless, as a mere coolie, but he had a remarkable career for all of that. He got into the good graces of a brigand chief, whose haunts were somewhere along the West River. The chieftain made him his Number One man, and when a few years later the old bandit died "unexpectedly" the Number One man proclaimed himself chief. . . . Thus he became respected and feared among the seafaring merchantmen along the South China coast, made a goodly amount of money, and collected junks as one collects stamps or Chinese porcelain. . . . The fishing junks—several hundreds of them—each paid a certain amount of money as long as he guaranteed that no other pirate would harass them in their lawful pursuit of livelihood.

The reporter learned that Lai Choi San had been married twice and had two sons. She confided that she wanted the older boy to become a rich rice merchant and go to America. The younger child, only five years old, was already "in training on another of her junks. One day, he was going to inherit all her ships and the 'trade.'"

The last reported battle of Lai Choi San involved an assault against a Japanese torpedo squadron during the late 1930s. The journalist Robert de la Croix described the battle:

> On the one side there were Japanese torpedo boats of the modern sort. . . . On the other side were simple ships similar to those that could be found along the Chinese coast all during the last two hundred years: junks and dragon boats with strange sails. The bows rose high out of the water, the sterns were provided with openings through which the cannons protruded. Some . . . were remnants from the 1904 Russo-Japanese war. There were also German machine guns from 1914; and American revolvers alongside English rifles from 1812. There was even a still-older weapon found, a French piece that was dated to 1798. . . . These pirate ships were a swimming museum.

Unable to defend against the powerful torpedoes, Lai Choi San's junks were defeated and sunk. De la Croix's report concluded solemnly, "The next day the news spread throughout the taverns and game halls of [Macao]. It was reputed to be a huge disaster. Not only did the entire fleet now lie on the ocean floor, but its captain had gone down with it."

Whether Lai Choi San actually died in this battle is a subject of controversy. According to other sources, she was taken prisoner and tried in 1939, and the International Coast Guard in Shanghai sentenced her to life in prison. The truth of her fate may never be known, but her story and her legend live on.

Since Lai Choi San's time, China's growing economy

has spawned a new wave of sophisticated sea piracy. The new sea wolves run organized criminal syndicates, making tens of thousands of dollars a year from what are known as "phantom ships" with fake names. The booty is no longer spices, silks, and gold, but easily disposable goods from electronics to cash. Once out at sea, the stolen ship is repainted, renamed, and the illegal cargo sold.

The swashbuckling days of men and women pirates remain a haunting shadow of the past. But as long as the lure of easy money and adventure on the high seas exists, piracy in some fashion may never be completely eradicated from the maritime world.

TIMELINE

1893	Mao Zedong (founder of the People's Republic of China) is born.
1900	The Boxer Rebellion takes place in China.
1917	China enters World War I on the side of the Allies.
1918	World War I ends.
1921	The Chinese Communist Party is founded.
1926	Civil war erupts in China.
1931	Mao Zedong is elected chairman of the new Soviet Republic of China.
1939	World War II begins; Lai Choi San may have been taken prisoner and tried in court.
1949	The People's Republic of China is established, with Mao at its head.

GLOSSARY

Acumen: Ability to be discerning, to see the point of things.

Amnesty: A pardon, usually offered to a large group of people.

Ballast: A heavy substance used to lend stability.

Becalmed: Kept motionless without wind.

Blacking boots: Shining shoes.

Booty: A rich gain or plunder taken.

Breeches: Short pants, reaching about to the knee, where they are snug.

Brig: A two-masted ship with square rigging.

Brigand: A robber or bandit.

Calico: A kind of cotton cloth, often decorated with patterns.

Cambric: A fine linen fabric.

Cartography: The science or art of map making.

Chantey: A song sung by sailors in rhythm to their work.

Cutlass: A short, curved sword used mainly by sailors.

Cutter: A small boat.

Dinghy: A small boat usually kept aboard a larger one.

Doubloon: A Spanish gold coin.

Flog: To whip.

Fringe: A British terms for bangs, or hair cut to hang above the eyes.

Galleon: A large ship with distinctive square rigging, used mainly by the Spanish.

Galley: An open ship or boat propelled mainly by oars.

Gallows: A frame from which criminals are hanged.

Garrison: A military post or the troops stationed there.

Gibbet: An upright post with an extension for hanging.

Grapnel: A small anchor with curved protrusions.

Guinea: An English coin, now worth twenty-one shillings.

Gunwale: The edge of a ship's side.

Impress: To force into service.

Junk: A ship typical of China.

Laudanum: A solution of opium, once used as a sleep aid.

Log: The record kept of a ship's progress and voyage.

Mainmast: The principal mast of a sailing ship.

Man-of-war: A warship of a recognized navy (as opposed to a pirate ship).

Maritime: Of, relating to, or bordering on the sea.

Pieces of eight: A slang term for Spanish coins.

Poop: A partial deck, usually enclosed, sitting above the main deck of a ship.

Prize: A captured ship.

Quay: A dock parallel to a waterway, used as a landing place.

Rattan: A climbing palm tree with tough stems, or a piece taken from the same.

Salver: A serving tray.

Sampan: A flat-bottomed skiff, usually propelled by oars.

Schooner: A kind of two-masted sailing ship.

Scrimshaw: A carved artifact usually made from whale ivory.

Shilling: A former English monetary unit.

Shipping lanes: Channels used by ships with heavy cargo.

Slavers: Ships carrying slaves.

Sloop: Smaller than a schooner, a sloop also has two masts but fewer sails.

Sovereign: An English gold coin.

Sphinx: Something enigmatic or mysterious.

Syndicate: A group of people who combine to control a market.

Tallow: Rendered animal fat used in candle making.

Trews: A term for pants.

Trousseau: The household goods and clothing a bride brings to a marriage.

Windlass: A barrel turned with a crank used for hoisting (in this case a sail).

SOURCES

ALFHILD

p. 13-14, "There were some . . ." Jo Stanley, ed., *Bold in Her Breeches: Women Pirates Across the Ages* (London: Pandora, 1995), 88-89.

p. 15, "who showed almost . . . close keeping," Ibid., 82.

p. 15, "wonderful dazzling glow . . ." Ibid.

p. 15, "that he would accept . . ." Ibid., 83.

p. 15, "stiff against the wooer's . . ." Ibid.

p. 15, "warmly praised . . . charming looks," Ibid.

p. 15, "Thus Alfhild was led . . ." Ibid.

p. 15, "many maidens who . . ." Ibid., 83.

p. 16, "happened to come . . ." Ibid., 84.

p. 16, "did deeds beyond . . ." Ibid.

p. 16, "many toilsome voyages," Ibid.

p. 16, "crossed the frozen . . ." Ibid.

p. 18, "leapt on Alfhild's prow . . ." Ibid., 85.

p. 18, "seeing the smoothness . . ." Ibid.

p. 18, "the woman whom . . ." Ibid.

p. 18, "her man's apparel . . ." Ibid.

p. 18, "wedded the attendant . . ." Ibid.

p. 18, "maidens of . . ." Ibid., 90.

GRACE O'MALLEY

p. 21, "the great spoiler . . ." Anne Chambers, "The Pirate Queen of Ireland: Grace O'Malley," in *Bold in Her Breeches,* ed. Jo Stanley, (London: Pandora, 1995), 96.

p. 21-22, "exploration and discovery . . ." Anne Chambers, *Granuaile: The Life and Times of Grace O'Malley* (Dublin, Ireland: Wolfhound Press, 1994), 9.

p. 25-26, "swarthy, broad-shouldered . . ." Chambers, "The Pirate Queen of Ireland," 98.

p. 28, "maintenance by land . . ." Ibid., 99.

p. 28, "Outenduring and outdoing . . ." Ibid., 101.

p. 29, "Skin toughened under . . ." Ibid., 100.

p. 29, "one year certain," Chambers, *Granuaile,* 77.

p. 29, "I dismiss you," Ibid., 78.

p. 30, "May you be seven-times . . ." Ibid.

p. 30, "the most feminine . . ." Chambers, "The Pirate Queen of Ireland," 102.

p. 31, "a broad interpretation . . ." Ibid., 103.

p. 31, "caused a new pair . . ." Ibid., 104.

p. 31, "manned out her navy . . ." Ibid.

p. 33-34, "aged woman," Chambers, *Granuaile,* 151.

p. 34, "quarrel with all . . ." Ibid.

p. 34, "maintenance by land . . ." Ibid.

p. 34, "famous for her stoutness . . ." David Cordingly, *Under the Black Flag* (New York: Random House, 1995), 72.

LADY KILLIGREW

p. 37, "so general as to be . . ." Patrick Pringle, *Jolly Roger: The Story of the Great Age of Piracy* (New York: W. W. Norton, Inc., 1953), 24.

p. 38, "gentleman pirate," Ibid., 28.

p. 38, "leading attacks in the same . . ." Stanley, *Bold in Her Breeches,* 118.

p. 40, "vultures preying . . ." Ibid.

p. 40, "above taking the boarding axe . . ." Ulrike Klausmann, Marion Meinzerin, and Gabriel Kuhn, *Women Pirates and the Politics of the Jolly Roger* (Montreal: Black Rose Books, 1997), 147.

p. 40, "finest and most costly," R. N. Worth, "The Family of Killigrew," *Journal of the Royal Institution of Cornwall* 12 (April 1871): 272.

p. 40-41, "which the pirates . . ." Klausmann, *Women Pirates,* 147.

p. 48, "lamented nothinge more . . ." H. Michell Whitley, "Dame Killigrew and the Spanish Ship," *Journal of the Royal Institution of Cornwall* (July 1883): 283.

MARIA COBHAM

p. 51, "the ocean groaned . . ." Albert Marrin, *The Sea King: Sir Francis Drake and His Times* (New York: Simon & Schuster, 1995), 119.

MARY READ

p. 63, "Milord, we plead our bellies," Jenifer Marx, *Pirates and Privateers of the Caribbean* (Malabar, FL: Krieger Publishing Company, 1992), 253.

p. 64, "as strange a blend . . ." Pringle, *Jolly Roger,* 218.

p. 64, "it might be thought . . ." Daniel Defoe, *A General History of the Pyrates,* ed. Manuel Schonhorn (originally published as Captain Charles Johnson, *A General History of the Robberies and Murders of the Most Notorious Pyrate*s (1724)) (Columbia: University of South Carolina Press, 1972), 130.

p. 64, "young and airy," Ibid.

p. 66, "Growing bold and strong . . ." Ibid., 131.

p. 67, "She behaved herself . . ." Ibid.

p. 67, "the esteem of all . . ." Ibid.

p. 68, "Two troopers, marrying . . ." Ibid., 132.

p. 73, "No Prey, No Pay," Joseph B. Feder, *Pirates* (New York: Mallard Press, 1992), 28.

p. 74, "They eat in a very . . ." Edward Smith-Lucie, *Outcasts of the Sea* (New York: Paddington Press LTD, 1978), 207.

p. 74, "with the fruits . . ." Charles Ellms, *The Pirates Own Book* (Salem, MA: Marine Research Society, 1924), 420.

ANNE BONNY

p. 77, "confirmed in all wicked . . ." John Carlova, *Mistress of the Seas* (New York: The Citadel Press, 1964), 244.

p. 77, "A more delectable . . ." Ibid., 12.

p. 79, "a fierce and couragious . . ." Philip Gosse, *The Pirates' Who's Who: Giving Particulars of the Lives & Deaths of the Pirates & Buccaneers* (Glorieta, NM: The Rio Grande Press, 1988), 202.

p. 79, "turned her out of Doors," Defoe, *A General History,* 165.

p. 83, "None among Rackam's . . ." Defoe, *A General History,* 133.

p. 84, "as good a marriage . . ." Ibid., 135.

p. 84, "most generous Actions . . ." Ibid., 134.

p. 88, "come up and fight . . ." Ibid., 133.

p. 88-89, "that to hanging . . ." Ibid., 135-136.

p. 89, "they had both resolved . . ." Ibid., 135.

p. 89, "special Favour . . ." Ibid., 141.

p. 89, "sorry to see him there . . ." Ibid.

p. 89, "for a publick Example . . ." Mendel Peterson, *The Funnel of Gold* (Boston: Little, Brown and Company, 1975), 426.

p. 90, "The two women prisoners . . ." Cordingly, *Under the Black Flag,* 64.

p. 90, "Anne Bonny, one of . . ." Peterson, *The Funnel of Gold,* 426, 429.

p. 91, "the said sentence . . ." Ibid., 429.

RACHEL WALL

p. 94, "honest and reputable," Rachel Wall, "Life, Last Words and Dying Confession of Rachel Wall," *Boston Goal,* October 7, 1789 (Columbia: University of South Carolina, Evans Early American Imprint microcard series, No. 22235).

p. 94, "They . . . taught me . . ." Ibid.

p. 95, "was received by them . . ." Ibid.

p. 95, "lived very contented," Ibid.

p. 96, "as soon as he came . . ." Ibid.

p. 101, "on my entering the cabin . . ." Ibid.

p. 101-102, "I looked round to . . ." Ibid.

p. 102, "I . . . declare Miss . . ." Ibid.

p. 103, "without design to injure . . ." Ibid.

p. 104, "she feloniously did assault . . ." Ibid.

p. 104, "And now into the . . ." Ibid.

FANNY CAMPBELL

p. 107, "I possess knowledge . . ." Edward Rowe Snow, *True Tales of Pirates and Their Gold* (New York: Dodd, Mead & Company, 1966), 163.

p. 107, "Come on, Charles . . ." Ibid.

p. 108, "A number of brave . . ." Wesley Griswold, *The Night the Revolution Began: The Boston Tea Party* (Brattleboro, VT: The Stephen Greene Press, 1972), 95.

p. 114, "Captain Brownless, you . . ." Snow, *True Tales of Pirates and Their Gold,* 168.

p. 114, "Mutiny!" Ibid.

p. 118, "an astonishing greenish-yellow . . ." Gail B. Stewart, *The Revolutionary War* (San Diego, CA: Lucent Books, 1991), 74.

CHENG I SAO

p. 121, "The pirates are too powerful . . ." Richard Platt, *Pirate* (New York: Alfred A Knopf, 1994), 54.

p. 123, "of the tint of rich . . ." Joseph Gollomb, *Pirates Old and New* (New York: The Macaulay Company, 1928), 98.

p. 123, "before the beauty . . ." Dian H. Murray, "Cheng I Sao in fact and fiction," in *Bold in Her Breeches,* ed. Jo Stanley, 218.

p. 126, "wretched," Ibid., 227.

p. 126-127, "At night the space . . ." Ibid.

p. 127, "I saw one man . . ." David Cordingly and John Falconer,

Pirates: Fact and Fiction (New York: Artabas, 1992), 108.

p. 127, "embroidered dragons . . . war helmet," Gollomb, *Pirates Old and New,* 279.

p. 127, "Look at me . . . other chief," Ibid.

p. 128, "liked him so much . . ." Murray, "Cheng I Sao in fact and fiction," 221.

p. 129, "have no settled residence . . ." Ellms, *The Pirates Own Book,* 296.

p. 129, "a small berth . . . of vermin," Ibid.

p. 130, "great delicacies," Ibid.

p. 130, "very few creatures," Ibid.

p. 130, "During our captivity . . ." Ibid.

p. 130, "much addicted to . . . opium," Ibid.

p. 130, "was very beautiful . . ." Murray, "Cheng I Sao in fact and fiction," 229.

p. 130, "the pirate dragged . . . drowned," Ibid.

p. 131, "which they were . . ." Ellms, *The Pirates Own Book,* 285.

p. 131-132, "melancholy sight to see . . ." Ibid.

p. 132, "twenty of the female . . ." Gollomb, *Pirates Old and New,* 290.

p. 132, "leaped over-board . . ." Stanley, *Bold in Her Breeches,* 230.

p. 132, "drawn sword in his hand . . . heads," Ellms, *The Pirates Own Book,* 290.

p. 132, "a miserable captivity . . ." Richard Glasspoole, *Mr. Glasspoole and the Chinese Pirates* (London: Golden Cockerel Press, 1935), 53.

p. 133, "leading a peaceful life . . ." Dian H. Murray, *Pirates of the South China Coast 1790-1810* (Stanford, CA: Stanford University Press, 1987), 150.

LAI CHOI SAN

p. 135, "twisted in a knot," Klausmann, *Women Pirates,* 56.

p. 136, "The Chinese pirates . . ." Stanley, *Bold in Her Breeches,* 242.

p. 136, "European clothes . . ." Ibid.

p. 136, "beating of the gongs," Ibid.

p. 137, "Here was I . . ." Aleko E. Lilius, *I Sailed with Chinese Pirates* (Oxford: Oxford University Press, 1930), 38.

p. 137-138, "Undoubtedly she is the Queen . . ." Ibid., 39.

p. 138, "was actually tramping . . ." Ibid., 40.

p. 138, "These fellows were . . ." Ibid., 41.

p. 138, "The ammunition, both powder . . ." Ibid.

p. 140, "an ordinary grand . . ." Ibid., 43.

p. 140, "As soon as the junk . . ." Ibid., 45.

p. 140, "Apparently, the business . . ." Ibid., 46.

p. 140-141, "an empty packing case . . ." Ibid., 43.

p. 141, "the captain's smile . . ." Ibid., 46.

p. 142, "The whole junk shook . . ." Ibid., 50.

p. 142, "the sinking hull . . ." Ibid.

p. 142, "actually saw the captain . . ." Ibid., 52.

p. 143, "Her father had four sons . . ." Ibid., 53.

p. 143, "in training on another . . ." Ibid., 56.

p. 144, "On the one side . . ." Klausmann, *Women Pirates,* 58.

p. 144, "The next day the news . . ." Ibid., 59.

BIBLIOGRAPHY

American Heritage. *Pirates of the Spanish Main.* New York: American Heritage Publishing Co., Inc., 1961.

Botting, Douglas. *The Pirates.* New York: Time-Life Books, Inc., 1978.

Brooke, Henry K. *Book of Pirates.* Philadelphia: J. B. Perry, 1847.

Carlova, John. *Mistress of the Seas.* New York: The Citadel Press, 1964.

Chambers, Anne. *Granuaile: The Life and Times of Grace O'Malley.* Dublin, Ireland: Wolfhound Press, 1994.

——————. "The Pirate Queen of Ireland: Grace O'Malley." In *Bold in Her Breeches.* Edited by Jo Stanley. London: Pandora, 1995.

Cordingly, David. *Under the Black Flag.* New York: Random House, 1995.

Cordingly, David and John Falconer. *Pirates: Fact and Fiction.* New York: Artabas, 1992.

Defoe, Daniel. *A General History of the Pyrates.* Edited by Manuel Schonhorn. (Originally published as Captain Charles Johnson, *A General History of the Robberies and Murders of the Most Notorious Pyrates* (1724)) Columbia, SC: University of South Carolina Press, 1972.

De Pauw, Linda Grant. *Seafaring Women.* Boston: Houghton Mifflin Company, 1982.

Ellms, Charles. *The Pirates Own Book.* Salem, MA: Marine Research Society, 1924.

Elton, Oliver, trans. *The First Nine Books of the Danish History of Grammaticus.* London: David Nutt, 1894.

Feder, Joseph B. *Pirates.* New York: Mallard Press, 1992.

Foster, R. F., ed. *The Oxford Illustrated History of Ireland.*

Oxford: Oxford University Press, 1989.

Glasspoole, Richard. *Mr. Glasspoole and the Chinese Pirates.* London: Golden Cockerel Press, 1935.

Gollomb, Joseph. *Pirates Old and New.* New York: The Macaulay Company, 1928.

Gosse, Philip. *The Pirates' Who's Who: Giving Particulars of the Lives & Deaths of the Pirates & Buccaneers.* Glorieta, NM: The Rio Grande Press, Inc., 1988.

Griswold, Wesley. *The Night the Revolution Began: The Boston Tea Party.* Brattleboro, VT: The Stephen Greene Press, 1972.

Keller, Allan. *Colonial America.* New York: Hawthorn Books, 1971.

Klausmann, Ulrike, Marion Meinzerin, and Gabriel Kuhn, *Women Pirates and the Politics of the Jolly Roger.* Montreal: Black Rose Books, 1997.

Lilius, Aleko E. *I Sailed with Chinese Pirates.* Oxford: Oxford University Press, 1930.

Manthorpe, Jonathan. "Asian Gangs Use 'Phantom Ships' to Steal Cargo: Growing Economy in China Fuels Sophisticated Sea Piracy by Organized Crime." *Vancouver Sun,* May 4, 1995, A 22.

Marley, David F. *Pirates.* Santa Barbara, CA: ABC-CLIO, Inc. 1994.

Marrin, Albert. *The Sea Rovers.* New York: Atheneum, 1984.

————. *The Sea King: Sir Francis Drake and His Times.* New York: Simon & Schuster, 1995.

Marx, Jennifer. *Pirates and Privateers of the Caribbean.* Malabar, FL: Krieger Publishing Company, 1992.

Matthew, David. "Cornish and Welsh Pirates in the Reign of Elizabeth." *English Historical Review* XXXIX (July 1924).

Mitchell, David J. *Pirates.* London: Thames & Hudson Ltd., 1976.

Murray, Dian H. *Pirates of the South China Coast 1790-1810.* Stanford, CA: Stanford University Press, 1987.

O'Brien, William. *A Queen of Men.* London: T. Fisher Unwin, 1898.

Peterson, Mendel. *The Funnel of Gold.* Boston: Little, Brown and Company, 1975.

Poertner, Rudolf. *The Vikings.* Translated by Sophie Wilkins. London: St. James Press, 1971.

Pringle, Patrick. *Jolly Roger: The Story of the Great Age of Piracy.* New York: W.W. Norton, Inc., 1953.

Platt, Richard. *Pirate.* New York: Alfred A. Knopf, 1994.

Rogozinski, Jan. *Pirates! Brigands, Buccaneers, and Privateers in Fact, Fiction, and Legend.* New York: Facts On File, Inc., 1995.

Smith-Lucie, Edward. *Outcasts of the Sea.* New York: Paddington Press LTD, 1978.

Snow, Edward Rowe. *True Tales of Pirates and Their Gold.* New York: Dodd, Mead & Company, 1966.

Stanley, Jo, ed. *Bold in Her Breeches: Women Pirates Across the Ages.* London: Pandora, 1995.

Stewart, Gail B. *The Revolutionary War.* San Diego, CA: Lucent Books, 1991.

Wall, Rachel. "Life, Last Words and Dying Confession of Rachel Wall." *Boston Goal,* October 7, 1789. Evans Early American Imprint microcard series, No. 22235. Columbia, SC: University of South Carolina.

Whitley, H. Michell. "Dame Killigrew and the Spanish Ship." *Journal of the Royal Institution of Cornwall,* July 1883.

Worth, R. N. "The Family of Killigrew." *Journal of the Royal Institution of Cornwall* 12 (April 1871).

Yolen, Jane. *The Ballad of the Pirate Queens.* San Diego, CA: Harcourt Brace & Co., 1995.

Yunglun, Yuen. *Ching hai-fen chi.* Translated by Charles Fried Neumann as *History of the Pirates Who Infested The China Sea from 1807 to 1810* (London: J. Murray, 1831).

WEB SITES

http://www.piratemuseum.com/pirate.htm
The online home of the New England Pirate Museum, located in Salem, Massachusetts.

http://www.blackbeardlives.com/
A fun, interactive site with lots of audio and video clips, sponsored in part by the Greensboro *News & Record.*

http://www.talklikeapirate.com/
John Baur and Mark Summers, with help from humor columnist Dave Barry, have created Talk Like a Pirate Day. Their site has links, news, and lots of information about how to talk like a pirate every September 19.

http://www.blackbeardfestival.com/
The Blackbeard Festival is held every year in Hampton, Virginia.

http://www.inkyfingers.com/pyrates/index.html
A fun site with great information about pirate history as well as lots of pictures of pirate ships, weapons, and flags.

INDEX

Alf, prince of Denmark, 15-16, 18-19, *19*

Alfhild, 8, 11-19, *17, 19*
   Marriage, 18

Barnet, Jonathan, 86-87

Belden, John Austin, 107-108, 119

Bingham, Richard, 31-33

Blackbeard, 80

Bonny, Anne Cormac, 63, 75, 77-80, 82-83, 85-91,
   Born, 78
   Marriage, 79

Bonny, James, 79-80, 82

Bourke, Richard-in-Iron, 29-31, 35

Boston Tea Party, 108, *109,* 119

Bowden, Elizabeth, 47-48

Boxer Rebellion, 145

Breed, Henry, 111, 115

Brennan, Peg, 78-79

Brownless, Captain, 114-115

Burnet, Robert, 109, 113, 116-117

Campbell, Fanny, 108-110, 113-119
   as Channing, 114-115
   Marriage, 118

Charles IX, king of France, 42

Chang Pao, 127-128, 132-133

Chavis, Juan de, 43, 45-47

Cheng I, 123-124, 127-128

Cheng I Sao (Hsi Kai), 9, 121-133, *125,* 135
   Death, 133
   First marriage, 123
   Second marriage, 128

Cobham, Eric, 51-61

Cobham, Maria Lindsey, 51-61
   Birth, 51
   Death, 60

Constance, 114-116

Cormac, William, 78-79

Cornwallis, Charles, 105, 119

Defoe, Daniel, 64, *64,* 68, 75, 88-89, 91

de la Croix, Robert, 144

Dillon, Thomas, 90

Drake, Francis, 22, 51, 61, 69

Elizabeth I, queen of England, 21-22, *22,* 27, 32-35, *33,* 37, 41-42, 47, 49, 61

French and Indian War, 93, 105

George, 115-116

George I, king of England, 75, 91

George III, king of England, 93, 105, 108, 119

Glasspoole, Richard, 129-133

Golden Age of Piracy, 9, 63, 70, 91

Gurid (Alfhild's daughter), 18

Hawkins, John, 43, 45-46, 48

Henry VIII, king of England, 41

Herbert, Jack, 111, 113-115

Hornigold, Ben, 80

Kendall, Henry, 43, 45-46, 48
Lady Killigrew, 38-49
Killigrew, Sir John, 38, 41-
    42, 45-46, 48-49

Lai Choi San, 135-145, *139*
    Death, 144
Lawes, Sir Nicholas, 77
Lilius, Alecko E., 137-138,
    140-142
Lovell, Charles Edward, 107-
    108
Lovell, William, 108-111,
    113, 115-116, 118-119

Mao Zedong, 145
Marie, 42-43, 45-46, 49
Marquis of Ely, 129
Mary II, queen of England, 75
Mei Ying, 130

O'Flaherty, Donal, 26-27, 35
O'Flaherty, Owen, 31, 35
O'Malley, Dudara, 22, 25-26
O'Malley, Grace, 21-35, *33, 37*
    Born, 22
    First marriage, 26
    Second marriage, 29
    Death, 34
O'Malley, Margaret, 22, 25
Oryo, Philip de, 43, 45-47

Philip II of Spain, 22

Rackam, "Calico" Jack, 74-
    75, 80-83, *81,* 85-86, 88-
    91, *90*
Raleigh, Walter, 22
Read, Mary, 63-68, 71-75, *66,*
    72, 76, 83-85, *85, 87,* 88-91
    Birth, 65
    Death, 91
    Marriage, 67-68
Revolutionary War, 93-94, 96,
    105, 117-119

Royal Kent, 109-111

Saxo Grammaticus, 11, 13, 15
Shakespeare, William, 22, 35
Sidney, Sir Henry, 30-31
Sigar, king of Denmark, 15-
    16
Siward, Viking king (Alfhild's
    father), 11, 15

Theobald of the Ships (also
Tibbot-na-Long), 30-31, 32
Thomas, Dorothy, 89-90
Turner, John, 125-127, *126,*
    133

Vane, Charles, 80

Wall, George, 95-100
Wall, Rachel, 93-105, *103*
    Birth, 93
    Death, 104
    Marriage, 95
War of the Spanish Succes-
    sion, 67, 75, 91
Washington, George, 105,
    118-119
William III, king of England, 75
Wolverton, Philip, 38
Woodes, Rogers, 74, 80, 82
World War I, 145
World War II, 145